KING VIDOR *on film making*

KING VIDOR
on film making

DAVID MCKAY COMPANY, INC.
NEW YORK

To Colleen
Who Insisted That I Write This Book

FOREWORD

Several years ago, I did an educational TV show with King Vidor. We had hired a car for the day, perched a cameraman on the front seat with an Arriflex camera, scrunched a sound man with a Nagra recorder at our feet, and drove all over the Hollywood that King loved and remembered, filming his recollections as we went. We passed a row of rather shabby frame houses, and he recalled that at one time he had rented just such a house, and had erected an open-air stage in its backyard. We drove through Griffith Park, and he showed us where he had staged the attack through the forest sequence for *The Big Parade*. "When we went on location in those days," he said with a grin that has never lost its youthfulness, "we always meant Griffith Park. The real problem was not getting somebody else's camera into your angle of vision."

Every once in a while, we would stop the car for something special, like the sprawling supermarket complex just south of where Hollywood Boulevard crosses Sunset. King climbed out, with camera accompaniment, and stretched his arms expansively. "Arthur," he said, "for me, this is where it all began. This was Griffith's studio when I arrived here in 1915, and over there"—he pointed across the boulevard toward some nondescript storefronts and a nudie house—"over there was the standing set for the Babylonian sequences of *Intolerance*." A few minutes later, we were at the site of King's own studio, built in the early twenties in the style of a Midwestern town of a decade or so earlier. It, too, had become a supermarket. "In fifty years, we've gone from superfilms to supermarkets," he grinned—only this time there was just a tinge of disappointment beneath the grin.

The disappointment, I suspect, is very much that of a man who has loved a woman all of his life, then late in life found her not that worthy. Incredibly, King Vidor's own life spans the entire history of motion pictures. (He was born, as a matter of fact, the year *before* the first movies were projected on a screen.) The love affair began early. At nine, he was wondering how to capture and preserve the movements of a group of boys clambering over a diving platform in his native Galveston, Texas, a scene that delighted his youthful eye because of the rhythm, the beauty, and the humor of its swirling action. Soon after, on a summer vacation from high school, he got his first movie job: ticket collector and part-time projectionist in Galveston's first movie house. By the time he was eighteen, King was working professionally, supplying newsreel material from Galveston to the motion picture "weeklies" in New York, and inventing little stories for local exposure. A year later, he was on his way to Hollywood with his beautiful bride, Florence, shooting travel footage for Ford Motors *en route* to finance the trip.

I have often been struck by how very young our film pioneers really were. King was twenty-four when he directed his first feature, *The Turn in the Road*. So was Chaplin when he began working for Keystone. Griffith was thirty-three when he started his directorial career at Biograph, and both Mack Sennett and Thomas H. Ince were barely thirty when they established their own studios. With the possible exception of Orson Welles, who made the redoubtable *Citizen Kane* at age twenty-five, the number of young people in our time who can look forward to directing a feature while still in their twenties is negligible. The medium has become too complex, the costs too high.

I think that this is one of the reasons why King Vidor wrote this book. The years of experience—and wisdom—that he has accumulated in a career that spans considerably more than half a century have been distilled here in an approach that uniquely combines philosophy and practicality. It is an approach that is desperately needed, particularly by young people hoping to make their way into films. The kind of direct experience that King and his contemporaries were able to garner in their daily encounters with the medium on the studio floor is no longer possible. Instead, today's young people can make their own mistakes on their own money, working on independent, low-budgeted, experimental productions—or they can go to a film school.

A film school is very much like a medical school or a law school. It takes the existing information about the field —the trials and errors as well as the triumphs—and compresses this into a manageable expanse of time. It offers opportunities for actual film making, but also classes in film theory and, above all, the opportunity to see again those classic works that, from time to time, reshaped existing patterns by introducing new styles and new techniques. The film school has, in effect, replaced the studio as the training ground for the next generation of film makers.

King is very much aware of this. Characteristically, in 1969 he went back to school, joining the faculty of the University of Southern California's Cinema Department as an artist in residence. In this capacity he supervised the creative work of the dozen or so graduate students who flocked to his classes. But he also returned with renewed vigor to his own experiments with the 16mm camera, finding in it the immediacy and intimacy that he had prized so much when he first began to work in films, but which the large studios—with their large crews—have steadily removed from professional production. At a time when

other directors many years his junior were languishing in
their Beverly Hills mansions, King was still exploring, still
experimenting in a medium that has never lost its fascination for him. Some of this is recounted in his chapter de-
voted to 16mm production.

I suspect, however, that his greatest source of satisfaction
today comes from the almost ceaseless stream of invitations
he receives to attend film festivals, to present retrospectives
of his works, or simply to address hordes of his admirers
in various parts of the world. An inveterate traveler, he
is more than apt to accept. I shall never forget his return
from Paris after one such event, when a number of his
pictures had been presented by the revered Cinemathèque
Française. This was followed by an open interview session
during which he was pelted with questions for several
hours. "Why," he said, with mingled pleasure and amaze-
ment, "they knew more about my pictures than I did!"

As a critic, I find it sad that King Vidor—still vigorous,
still alert, still creative—has not been permitted to direct
a feature film since his large-scale *Solomon and Sheba* in
1959. The sadness is not so much for him: He still lives a
rich, full life, alternating between Los Angeles, his beloved
ranch near Paso Robles, and his frequent travels, often
to exotic film festivals. (Even as I write this, he is off somewhere in the South Seas where, no doubt, someone is
holding a King Vidor Festival in Papeete.) The sadness
is for us, for it is we who are being deprived of a new
King Vidor film this year—and probably next year, and
the next. The industry has succumbed to the cult of the
young. An Old Master, by its lights, is merely a master
who is no longer youthful, not a man who has matured
to the point of creating his greatest works. As Richard
Griffith once wrote of Robert Flaherty, "it looks like a
plain waste of natural resources." And, in the case of
King, I can only agree.

I am not sure, however, that King would. I feel certain that he would like to do a studio film again, but only if it were the right one, and on his own terms. Meanwhile, he is still filled with his 16mm projects: a film on an old Scottish castle that friends of his have recently brought and renovated; a film recording the excitement of the Paso Robles locals staging their annual amateur show; his completed half-hour film on metaphysics, one of the enduring interests of his life. And I also think he is pleased that studio indifference has afforded him the opportunity to complete this book. It is a labor of love, a love that embraces the medium itself, and all of those who will follow him in practicing it. In it, he sets down no rules, erects no boundaries. It is, rather, the work of a world-famous director who remembers vividly that young novice back in Galveston in 1915 who threw a camera into the back of his Ford and set out to conquer Hollywood. What should he have known? What should he have done?

King Vidor on Film Making answers these questions for the novice of today. And in doing so, he has created a work that should be read not only for information, but for inspiration. It is, ultimately, a testament to the spirit that has energized the true film maker in every age, of every age, and in every part of the world. It is the work of an artist beckoning to every artist who will follow him into this most complex and most rewarding of all the arts today.

ARTHUR KNIGHT
LOS ANGELES
JUNE 1972

To Lynn Sonberg who edited the manuscript, to Nancy Dowd who supplied research material, and to Betty Hodgkinson who typed it, my sincere appreciation.

TABLE OF CONTENTS

I ON THE SET:
Artistic Freedom and the Studio System

■

CHAPTER 1

A BOOK FOR FILM MAKERS

$\boxed{\bullet}$

An Introduction is unnecessary in this book. Today we are all friends; movies have supplied us with a common ground. The subject I am going to talk about is as vital to everyone's life as milk and bread. You grew up with it. It affected your character, your dress, your love-making, your courage.

My name has been projected onto movie screens since the early twenties, and by the way, it *is* my real name. I had an uncle by the name of King. He was my mother's favorite brother. The Vidor is Hungarian. My grandfather emigrated to Texas in 1865. He was a press agent for a famous Hungarian violinist named Rimini.

Neither my grandfather nor my father had anything to do with the theater or show business before I came along: in fact, movies were born the same year that I was.

My first memory is of motion. I remember being intrigued by the pattern and rhythm of a group of boys climbing aboard and diving from three levels of a floating platform. As soon as the smaller boys crawled from the water they were on their feet, running across the platform and jumping into the water in a repetitious action that occurred every few seconds. The middle-sized boys climbed a few steps to a raised platform and either jumped or dove into the water. This action required about half a minute before repeating itself. The third and oldest group climbed

a ladder to a ten-foot stand where they stood, took deep
breaths to give them courage, raised their arms to a diving
position and pushed off. As they descended they seemed to
float in a slower rhythm than either of the other two
groups.

I was nine years old and I had just seen my first motion
picture.

I remember my father bought me a five dollar Brownie
camera (for singing in the church choir). I sold the
Saturday Evening Post and bought a developing outfit so
that I could develop and print my own films. In the next
six months I probably earned ten or twelve dollars taking
photographs of friends, relatives, and neighbors.

As far back as I can recall, I was interested in how things
worked and I started taking them apart to find out. I
subscribed to *Popular Mechanics* and *Scientific American*
and found some drawings in *Popular Mechanics* that explained the workings of a moving picture camera.

I was fascinated with the theater and got backstage
whenever I could find some excuse for doing so. In the
small town where I lived I had one job winding a windlass
that raised and lowered the curtain of a third-rate vaudeville show.

During vacation I got a job as ticket taker in the first
movie house in our town. Hours: 10:30 A.M. to 10:30 P.M.
Salary: $3.50 per week. I learned to operate the projection
machine while the regular projectionist went to lunch.

One day I met another youngster who was building a
movie camera out of parts of an old projection machine
and cigar boxes. When a tropical hurricane struck the
town, we went out to the ocean front and tried to capture
its fury. The day that hurricane struck the course of my
future was settled.

The universe can belong to anyone who owns a camera
and if it is a movie camera he will be able to tell everyone

all about his greatest possession—his vision of the world.

As we evolve into an era of conscious subjective reality, as we become convinced that all of life is an outpouring of conscious awareness, cinematography becomes the most complete medium of expression. A few years ago Christopher Isherwood wrote a play which he called *I Am a Camera*. This is an intriguing idea as it expresses a profound truth. A camera observes, records, and, guided by the individual, interprets everything. I, as existing, conscious man do all that the camera does, but in addition I am able to reverse the process of absorption and express all that I am capable of perceiving. Therefore, the movie camera becomes my most useful tool.

With the evolution of technology, man began to express the hope that he would be able to capture the passing moments and preserve them for posterity. He wanted to relive them and enjoy them again whenever he felt like it. But this was not the sole motivation of his quest.

To the painter, the sketcher, or the engraver, had fallen the task of recording the present. He had a medium of self-expression: through line, color, and form, he could give shape to some of the feelings his individuality needed to express. He could speak beyond the limits of documentation; he could speak as an artist.

The need, however, was for both a more precise instrument and a more expansive one; one that could overcome the limitations of color-bearing oil, of charcoal, or of a sharp, pointed stylus.

I doubt that the early experimenters in photography or cinema were wholly conscious of this goal of individual expression, but it was there. I doubt that the early operators of the cine cameras knew what a giant medium of self-expression they were cranking up. With each roll of film that clicked through the box, this powerful giant was struggling for release.

The first day I started teaching a class in film directing at the University of Southern California a young student in the group of twelve asked me what I considered the most important thing one must learn in becoming a director. I thought about my reply for a few moments and then told him that the most important thing to learn was to be an individual. Each individual sees his world from a slightly different viewpoint. It is this personal interpretation of the world around him that gives interest to what the individual artist has to say. One of the most difficult jobs for the aspiring artist of any sort is to find out exactly who he is. The medium of expression, the canvas and oils, the paper and pens, the motion picture camera, the piano, or the ballet stage, take their place in a necessary yet secondary position. They are the tools which the craftsman-artist uses to communicate. He should learn their function and possibilities thoroughly so that his ideas will not be stifled nor burdened by lack of what is generally known as technical efficiency.

So, throughout this book we will lay stress upon the importance of the individual and his particular viewpoint no matter where our discussion of technical proficiency seems to lead.

It all began about 1831 when a French painter named Louis Jacques Daguerre first experimented with sensitizing silver plates which he fumed with iodine vapors to form a layer of silver iodide. These plates were exposed in a camera obscura for several hours in order to produce a visible image. A camera obscura was a box or a room with a pin-hole on one side which acted as a lens. This pin-hole orifice projected the exterior image across the room to a flat surface on the opposite side. For several years Daguerre tried in various ways to shorten the required exposure time until finally, in 1837, he found that images could be obtained on plates with only a few minutes' exposure provided the plate was subjected to the fumes of mercury after the exposure. The process was described by Francois Arago at a meeting of the Paris Academy of Science and the French government gave a life pension to Daguerre on condition that the invention be made public without patent.

The making of Daguerreotypes became very popular in many countries including the United States. Exposures were shortened to a matter of seconds by the use of silver bromide and by the introduction of the portrait lens.

While Daguerre was working hard to improve his process, an Englishman, William H. F. Talbot, began experimenting independently on ways of sensitizing paper for use in the camera obscura.

Several months before Daguerre's process was made public, Talbot read a short paper and showed examples of his work at a meeting of the Royal Society in London. However, Talbot was fully aware of the shortcomings of his process and worked intensively to overcome them. In the fall of 1840 he made an important advance when he discovered a method of developing the latent image.

Since Talbot's method included all the elements of photography as it is known today—that is, exposure and development of an image to form a negative from which a positive is printed—Talbot, along with Daguerre, must be recognized as the discoverer of modern photography.

During these early experiments, only sensitized metal or paper was used. Because of the inherent grain of paper, a substitute material was sought. In 1847 Claude De Saint Victor succeeded in coating glass with egg white (albumen) as the carrier for the silver iodide.

Dry plates were marketed in several countries including the United States and these new materials needed ten times less exposure time than wet plates. Cameras designed for dry plate exposure were usually of the field type mounted on tripods or movable stands. Around the turn of the century, simple portable box cameras were marketed and photography came into wider use.

The development of photography as used today came about largely through the work of George Eastman (1854–1932), a manufacturer of dry plates at Rochester, New York. In 1883 to 1884 he developed the method of photography now known as the roll film system.

A syrupy solution was poured onto long glass tables, allowed to dry, coated with a substratum of silicate and finally, with the sensitive emulsion. When dry, the film was cut into various widths and lengths and wound on spools. Some of this film was supplied to the American inventor Thomas A. Edison in August 1889, who used it in connection with his experiments with the Kinetoscope, forerunner of the motion picture camera. Patents were granted Eastman and his chemist Henry N. Reichenbach in 1889 for the development of this flexible film and for the equipment needed in the manufacturing process.

The basic conditions of photography were changed profoundly by Eastman's introduction of flexible film. Thousands of individuals who had never been interested in photography were now encouraged to take it up as a hobby.

The introduction and marketing of flexible film, which could be cut into long strips and made into rolls, paved the way for the invention of the motion picture camera. Men had been making devices as a result of the desire to analyze the motion of various animals. Previous to 1890, such men as Etienne Jules Marey (France), Eadweard Muybridge (United States), and Louis A. A. Le Prince (England), were developing such machines. Their devices can be regarded as the precursors of the motion picture camera. Cameras, somewhat like those used today, were designed almost concurrently by Thomas A. Edison and William Kennedy Dickson in the United States; Louis Jean Lumière in France; William Friese-Greene and later Robert W. Paul in England and Oskar Messter in Germany. Thomas Armat (1866–1948) of Washington, D.C., is generally regarded as the father of the motion picture projector. (His version of the machine was developed in 1895.)

The motion picture camera is a simple but ingenious machine. A mechanism moves a strip of film past an aperture in a rapid series of stops and starts. This aperture or window sits directly behind a lens which is very similar to the lens of one tube in a pair of binoculars or a small telescope and has the function of reducing all that it sees to a miniature image that can be contained in an area about the size of a postage stamp.

In addition to its condensing ability, the lens has two other principal functions. One is the ability to focus what it sees on to the film so that the image is sharp and not blurred. (Remember that in the case of moving picture film the miniature image must be sufficiently precise to withstand enlargement by approximately 75,000 times when projected onto the theater screen. Any error in registration would be multiplied proportionally.) The lens must also be able to control the intensity of light or brightness passing through it so that the recorded image is not over- or underexposed—that is, not too dark or too light.

The light control is effected by a series of semicircular thin black sheets overlapping in the form of an iris flower. Its technical name is "iris-diaphram" and it is controlled by a ring on the outer surface of the lens complex. It is capable of being opened to a full circle whose circumference is almost equal to the circumference of the lens itself or it can be stopped down to a size equivalent to the

size of a pencil lead. The words "stopped down" are used
because the dimensions of this iris-shaped opening are cali-
brated in figures called "ƒ-stops". Generally, they run from
ƒ/1.5 depending on the light transmission capability of the
lens to ƒ/22 designating the small pinhead opening. When
one first becomes interested in the workings of a camera,
he is puzzled that these figures seem to indicate a reverse
function, that is, small numbers for the larger openings
and large numbers for the small ones.

But this apparent contradiction is soon resolved and one
becomes aware that ƒ/22 is used for the brightest of scenes
—sunlight on sand, surf and snow—and ƒ/1.5 or/2 for sufficient light transmission during the late hours of the day,
in heavily shaded areas and for dimly lighted interiors.

The film itself is also capable of a wide scale of sensitivity. We will take this up in our discussion of film
qualities. Between the lens and the aperture holding the
film is a revolving screen or shutter. The function of this
part of the mechanism is to cut off the light image passing
through the lens while the film is passing from one frame
or registration to the next. This process presents a strange
paradox. Although the illusion of action of a movie scene
is most convincing, yet from a factual viewpoint the effect
of movement is purely illusionary. One of the progressive
steps in the development of the motion picture camera
was to perfect the absolute stillness of each frame during
its brief visit in the camera's aperture. In like manner, this
immovability holds true during the exposure of the frame
in the aperture of the projection machine as well. The
purpose of the revolving screen or shutter is to block out
the forward movement of the film in its travel from one
frame to the next. If any actual movement was seen,
blurred images passing the aperture would be the result.

The film (fed intermittently from the upper feed magazine to the exposure aperture and into the lower take-up

magazine) is manufactured in several widths and can have a wide variety of sensitivity to exposure light.

The most common widths are 8mm, super-8, 16mm, and 35mm. In rare instances 70mm film is used.

The selection of film width is governed by its ultimate use. Eight mm and super 8mm film and equipment is designed principally for the amateur because of its lower cost. It is limited in the size of the picture it can project and in the quality of its sound reproduction. The cost of buying the original camera, the film, and film processing is about half that of 16mm. Television broadcasters are not equipped to accept 8mm film for their programs. However, it is used in some universities and in high school cinema departments. These schools often have a library of classic films in 8mm on hand which the student can draw from, along with a light weight projector, for home study. The ease of transporting such light weight equipment is a plus factor in cinema studies and experimental film making, although its approach to professionalism cannot be compared with the next larger size—16mm.

The technical and aesthetic possibilities of 16mm film and equipment compare favorably, in every way, with the larger 35mm size used by almost all studios and professional film makers. Again, there is a great advantage in the cost of equipment, film, and processing over the wider 35mm film. The portability makes it an ideal size for small crews for the serious film maker in the field of documentaries, films for television, student films, news coverage, scientific research, travel, exploration, etc. There have been quite a number of full-length or feature films shot in 16mm which were then blown up to a 35mm negative from which 35mm prints could be successfully made. This blowing up process has been under experimentation for the past fifteen years and took a big step forward with the development of the "wet-gate" process. The goal is to produce a 35mm negative that has all the quality of the original 16mm negative without developing graininess in the transition. The film *Woodstock* was shot with a dozen or more 16mm cameras and then transformed into a 35mm negative for world-wide distribution. In the last year or so there has been developed, principally in Europe, a super 16 film which is expected to overcome some of the problems in this blowing up process. It has the same relationship to 16mm that super 8 has to 8mm. The main disadvantage is that only one or two of the many 16mm cameras now in use can be adapted to this new film.

The leading 16mm cameras are the Arriflex (Germany), Eclair, and Beaulieu (France), Bolex (Switzerland), Eastman, and Bell & Howell (United States) and Nikon (Japan). The first two are considered the most professional instruments and the next two following closely behind.

During travels in recent years in Europe, Russia, and the United States, I have noticed that the Arriflex camera and the Nagra tape recorder (Switzerland) were the most generally used by professionals. Evidently these two manufacturers put a perfection into their equipment that is universally recognized.

In the latter years of my work in directing silent film features, I was developing in my mind a plan which I felt would free my activities from the weight and complications of big studio operation with its consequent high, high overhead. Generally speaking the greater the production cost the less freedom there is to express oneself as an individual. A camel is a horse designed by a committee. Extremely high-budget pictures must be designed to fill large theaters and appeal to mob tastes rather than a selective audience.

I wanted to be able to carry all the equipment, lights, cameras, film, reflectors, etc., in the back of an automobile, or at most a station wagon. This would give me the flexibility to stop and set up a production unit wherever or whenever the location or the natural lighting looked favorable. I remembered my early days in Hollywood when the whole company had gone on location in one seven-passenger Packard automobile. At the time, I was the assistant director, and was expected to act as chauffeur as well. The director occupied the other front sea; then came the camera man and his assistant on the two folding jump seats, and in the rear seat the cast—two stars and a character man. The Bell and Howell camera was strapped to the running board on one side and the camera tripod on the other. Roped to the spare tire on the rear of the car was one silvered folding reflector, shiney on one side, dull on the other. If the director saw a maple tree alive with the golden hues of a late afternoon sun, he could stop, and while the cameraman and his assistant set up the equipment, ad lib a love scene that would later allow any theater organist to give vent to the full power of his romantic imagination.

On one such location trip in the silent picture days, I was driving; but next to me, instead of the director, was the star of the film, the then heavyweight champion of the world, Jack Dempsey. The director, on this trip in the back seat, spotted a hay field backed by a green knoll that appealed to him. Despite a sign near the wire gate that said "No Hunting or Trespassing", he told me to drive into the place. I had opened the gate and was driving in when across the field came running an irate farmer. He was calling out something like, "You blind bastards. Can't you read signs!"

I stopped the car and as he came closer he saw, by the two actors in pale makeup, that we were a moving picture crew. "That's it," he yelled, "a bunch of Hollywood actors. Turn this car around and get off my place or I'll kick you off one by one."

By this time, he had moved into a position where he had

both hands on the right front door of the open touring car with his face not eighteen inches away from that of the champion prize-fighter whom he was already beginning to recognize through the pale pink make-up.

I still remember the slow transformation. From my vantage point, the close-up view of the poor man's face has been a useful memory whenever I have had to photograph an actor in a similar situation.

"Why, Mr. Dempsey, I didn't know this was your car." Of course he didn't. "You want to take pictures on my farm? Anytime—it would be a pleasure. When did you turn movie star?" Dempsey, smiling, sat silent. Then to me, "Go ahead young man, it's a pretty farm and you can take pictures wherever you like."

So much for the flexibility of a small crew and portable equipment, especially if you have room in the front seat for the heavyweight champion of the world.

Then it was 1929. I was a victim of a large studio with two thousand telephones, a police and fire department, a mail department, camera department, laboratory, carpenter shops, plaster shop, wardrobe department, publicity department, commissary, barber shop, accounting, casting, and on and on, ad infinitum. This jumble all came under an overhead of four or five thousand dollars a day, very little of which actually went into the finished film. I dreamed about a portable outfit; and a few knowledgeable assistants traveling through India, or Mexico, or Japan, or Tahiti. Suddenly, we would come upon the nucleus for a story. The settings and the actors would all be there waiting. It might be a tribe, or a village; but we would dig out their saga, and we would come away with a completed film. It was a pleasant and exciting dream.

And then came synchronous sound recording!

In order to silence them, cameras went into huge icebox-like cabinets and sound engineers, who had been trained to stifle their emotions and imaginations, told you what

you could and couldn't do. Cameras couldn't pan or per-
ambulate; a low set-up or a high one was impossible. It
took sixteen men and a five-ton truck to move one of the
soundproof cabinets. Portability, flexibility, going on location in two or three automobiles, all took a temporary
leave of absence.

In the shooting of my first sound film (*Hallelujah,*
M.G.M., 1929) the studio had no portable sound equipment for use on location. Interestingly enough, this proved
to be a distinct advantage. The locations I had selected
were in and around Memphis, Tennessee, and across the
river into Arkansas's cotton fields and swamps. I con-
cluded that for all location shooting, we would have to
put the sound in afterward. This left us free to use the
camera and the action of the people before it in the same
manner we would have in the silent days. The big problem
arose later in the cutting room.

Sound films came upon Hollywood so rapidly that there
hadn't been time to develop editing equipment for syn-
chronizing the sound and picture tracks. We couldn't read
the lips of the actors to determine what words they were
saying, particularly in the long shots. I rigged a push-
button control from the projection room theater to a
flashing lamp in the projection booth. The operator was
instructed to make a grease pencil mark on the moving
film when the light flashed signaling the onset of line of
dialogue. Afterwards the editor and I would go to the
cutting room and try to synchronize the two tracks.

When we would return to the theater to view the sequence with sound, we would invariably find that the
synchronization was two to six feet off—the result of the
time it took for me to press the button and the operator to
reach into the mechanism of the projector with the mark-
ing pencil.

As portable sound equipment began to arrive, and

cameras, by the use of individual noise-proof coverings, escaped from their heavy, thick-walled prisons—and craft guilds and unions escalated their demands—the number of trucks, busses, and automobiles that it took to accomplish a location trip reached impractical proportions. (See photo 1 following page 82.) On one expedition, only half an hour from the studio, I counted one hundred three persons in the crew for two actors in front of the cameras. The scene was a simple one that called for the two leads to bid farewell on either side of a white picket gate. Imagine how many technicians would have been added had the scene called for rain, or snow, or wind, or if early technicolor had been used for the scene. Technicolor cameras, up until a few years ago, weighed 800 pounds and took about six men to move from one set-up to the next. (See photo 2.)

The following call sheets are from *Portnoy's Complaint,* being shot on location in Rome on Thursday, June 24, 1971. Rome was only one of the cities demanded by the shooting of this film. Other location stops were New York City, Dorset, Vermont, Israel, Athens, with headquarters and principal shooting done at Warner Bros. Studio in Burbank, California. The company had nine days of work in Rome, seven days in Israel, two weeks in Dorset, Vermont and two weeks in New York City. The entire shooting schedule was for seventy-five days and the total budget $4,500,000. Shooting was completed in eighty-one days, one week over the scheduled time, resulting in approximately $30,000 over on the budget.

The call sheet shown on the pages to follow was for some night scenes made on or near Via Veneto and Doney's famous restaurant and sidewalk cafe adjoining Hotel Excelsior where most of the cast and the principal members of the staff were staying. This proximity eliminated many of the problems as well as the cost of transportation.

Twelve actors are involved in the scene and the crew,

WARNER BROS. INC.

C A L L   S H E E T

DATE Thursday. 6.24.71.

PICTURE "PORTNOY'S COMPLAINT"   DIRECTOR ERNEST LEHMAN

SET EXT: Side Street - Via Veneto (N) Sc:152.PT.   LOCATION Via Campania,Rome

SET EXT: Via Veneto (Doney's) (N)   Sc:146/7PT.   LOCATION Via Veneto (Doney

SET   LOCATION

NAME	MAKEUP CALL	SET OR LEAVING CALL	WDRBE. CHG. NO.	CHARACTER, SCENE NO'S., ETC.
RICHARD BENJAMIN	7.30pm	8.00pm		ALEX
KAREN BLACK	6.30pm	8.00pm		MONKEY
FRANCESCA DE SAPIO	6.00pm	8.00pm		LINA
1). MARISA TRAVERSI)	6.00pm	8.00pm		
2). ANTONELLA DOGAN)	"	"		
3). ANNA CARDARELLA)	"	"		STREET WALKERS
4). PERI HAN)	"	"		
5). MAYA MORIN)	"	"		
6). PATRIZIA MARZOLLA)	"	"		
BRENDA VICARI	9.00pm	10.00pm		STREET WALKER AT CORNER
CATHERINE DOLAN	9.00pm	10.00pm		No.1. STREET WALKER
ANNIE EIDEL	9.00pm	10.00pm		No.2. SMILING STREET WALKER

ITALIAN CREW CALL 7.00pm.

EXTRAS AND PROPS:

LUCIANO PESCAROLI	Unit Manager	
PAOLO TASSARA	Prod.Asst.	
BRUNO PERRIA	Transport Manager	
LUCIANO SACRIPANTI	1st.Asst.	
MARIO JURISIC	2nd.Asst.	
LUCIANO FOTI	Crowd Marshall	
ARMANDO ZAPPI	" "	
ANNALISA NASALLI ROCCA	Wardrobe Lady	
EDWIGE FRANCHI	Seamstress	
BRUNA FINOCCHI	Seamstress	
FRANCO FUNAGALLI	Set Dresser	
GIUSEPPE TINELLI	Camera Asst.	
LUCARELLI LANFRANCO	" "	
ALDO DE MARTINO	Boom Man	
WALTER ZUCCHI	Cable Man	
LUCIANO MARROCCHI	Gaffer	5.30.pm.
ROMEO GIVERNATORI	Head Grip	"
STEFANO SCAROZZA	Makeup Man	"
M.LUISA GARBINI	Hairdresser	"
15 ELECTRICIANS		"
8 GRIPS		"
IVANO TODESCHI	Asst.Props	7.00.pm.

EXTRAS AND PROPS:

Standins - 3
10 Street - Atmos.
3 Atmos. Car Drivers
1 Motorcycle Driver
1 Car for Irate Driver
Alex Car No.2.
Cars to block road as
        discussed
Cars to block Doney's as
        discussed
Car jack as discussed
Police-Co-operation as
        discussed
LATER:

200 Extras as discussed
    Times as discussed
Head Waiter

4 Waiters

Food, drinks per Dennis
           Parrish.

Form 278

SIGNED Nucky Moore

ASSISTANT DIRECTOR

AMERICAN CREW CALL: 7.00pm.

ERNEST LEHMAN
RICHARD MOWHORTER
MICKY MOORE
PHIL LATHROP
BILL JOHNSON
JIM SONGER
DON HOWARD
MOSS MABRY
DENNIS PARRISH
MARIE KENNEY
CLIFF KING

LEE WILSON   5.30.pm.   CALL

CHARLES SCHRAMM   5.45.pm.   CALL

KAY POWNALL   5.45.pm.   CALL

WALLY JONES   6.00.pm.   CALL

ASSISTANT DIRECTOR

June 24th, 1971.

WARNER BROS. INC.

"PORTNOY'S COMPLAINT"

A M E R I C A N   C R E W   L I S T

SURNAME	Name	Qualification	Hotel & Room Number
MOWHORTER	Richard	Production Manager	Hotel EXCELSIOR 207-208
REED	Mildred	Secretary	Hotel EXCELSIOR 279
LATHROP	Phil	Cinematographer	Hotel EXCELSIOR 128-129
JOHNSON	Bill	Camera Operator	Hotel EXCELSIOR 364
KING	William	Camera Asst.	Hotel EXCELSIOR 136
SONGER	Jim	Sound Mixer	Hotel EXCELSIOR 439
HOWARD	Don	Recorder	Hotel EXCELSIOR
MABRY	Moss	Costume Designer	Hotel DE LA VILLE
JONES	Wally	2nd Asst.Director	Hotel EXCELSIOR 440
SCHRAMM	Charles	Make-up Man	Hotel EXCELSIOR
CRISS	Lamar	Auditor	Hotel EXCELSIOR
PARRISH	Dennis	Prop Master	Hotel EXCELSIOR 579
KENNEY	Marie	Script Supervisor	Hotel EXCELSIOR 379
WILSON	Lee	Gaffer	Hotel EXCELSIOR 336
POWNALL	Kaye	Hair Dresser	Hotel EXCELSIOR 466
MOORE	Mickey	1st Asst.Director	Hotel EXCELSIOR 437
BLACK	Karen	Actress	Hotel EXCELSIOR 119-120
DESAPIO	Francesca	Actress	Hotel EXCELSIOR 679
BENJAMIN	Richard	Actor	
LEHMAN	Ernest	Director	Hotel EXCELSIOR 419-420

Production office, Rooms 116-117   , Wardrobe Room 156, Make-up Rooms, 155-157-
Production, Accounting offices - Via Veneto 7, Telef.: 463.294

Rome, June 18th, 1971.

WARNER BROS. INC.

"PORTNOY'S COMPLAINT"   June 18th 1971

ITALIAN CREW LIST

SURNAME	Name	Qualification	Address	Phone
PESCIAROLI	Luciano	Unit Manager	Via Luigi Credaro 9	349.6181
TASSARA	Paolo	Prod.Asst.	Via Modigliani 34	513.1012
PERRIA	Bruno	Transport.Manager	Via Q.Varo 33.	990524/747.586
GNOLI	Mimi	Prod.Secretary	Via Arenula 16	657.450
RODI	Raoul	Prod.Acc.Cashier	Via A.Claudio 240	741.426
SACRIFANTI	Luciano	1st Asst. Director	Via F.Tiberio	304.729
JURISIC	Mario	2nd Asst. Director	Via F.Buono 109	540.0347
ROLLI	Paola	Casting Director	P.San S.Lauro 13	653.703
CELLI	Maria	Crowd Casting	Via M.Scevola 28	785.6860
KNOX	Mickey			641/757
FOTI	Luciano	Crowd Marshall	Via del Pini 14	215.251
ZAPPI	Armando	Crowd Marshall	Via V.Spurinna 147	766.0730
NASALLI ROCCA	Annalisa	Wardrobe Lady	Via R. Fauro 54	802.597
FRANCHI	Edwige	Seamstress	Via Acqui 23	743.979
FINOCCHI	Bruna	Seamstress	Via A.Claudio 240	741.425
FUMAGALLI	Franco	Set Dresser	Vicolo del Cedro 3	589.1773
TINELLI	Giuseppe	Camera Asst.	Via A.del Vecchio 65	523.5089
LANFRANCO	Lucarelle	Camera Asst.		634.964
DE MARTINO	Aldo	Boom Man	Via A.Claudio 239	748.0517
ZUCCHI	Walter	Cable Man	Via A.Claudio 282	747.0471
MARROCCHI	Luciano	Gaffer	Via C.Canuleio	748.2767
GOVERNATORI	Romeo	Head Grip	Via Albano 46	788.4543
SCAROZZA	Stefano	Make-Up Man	Via C.Pallavicini 21	527.0240
GARBINI	M.Luisa	Hair Dresser	Via del Commercio 12	577.1230
TODESCHI	Ivano	Asst. Propman		767.1029

Production offices at Excelsior Hotel Rooms 116-117, Wardrobe Room 156; Make up
Rooms 155-157, Production, Accountin offices at Via Veneto 7, Telephone; 453.294

besides the director, the production manager, and the cinematographer, is comprised of sixteen Americans and twenty-four Italians. There are also fifteen electricians and eight grips listed in the Italian crew call. I have listed nine street walkers, some of whom are probably only bit players, as principal actors. I have not at this writing seen the film, nor read the book.

Among the extras and props are three stand-ins, evidently for the three principals, Alex, Monkey and Lina. There are ten extras for street atmosphere, three atmosphere car drivers, and one motorcycle driver who have evidently been checked out by the director and/or the assistant director. In order to completely control the movement of the pedestrians on the sidewalks and those seated in and out of the cafe, two hundred extras and cooperation from the police have been requisitioned. For important night scenes with lights, cameras, mike booms and crew everywhere it would be impractical for the director and his assistants to try to control the movement and appearance of the normal pedestrians and cafe devotees. They would be looking into the camera lens, grinning self-consciously and hardly be amenable to doing a scene over and over until the director got the take he wanted.

You will note that the production office, wardrobe and make-up rooms are all nearby in the Hotel Excelsior with the accounting offices in the immediate vicinity on the Via Veneto. A very concise and efficient operation for a few days shooting in a foreign city. The big question here is whether the audience would be able to tell the difference if the Rome locale for the night scenes had been simulated in the back lot of the studio in California. I can't answer this until I have seen the film. No director prefers shooting on actual locations any more than I do. But besides the inherent inspiration there is always a feeling that because you are actually there the native smell and ambience will

rub off onto the film. True of daytime full shots or shots
where backgrounds or streets, buildings and monuments
are part of the story, but the depth of artificial lighting on
exterior night scenes is not very great. Still in all, the sur-
roundings might make the director feel very much more
confident and at ease, so I will keep my mouth shut.

I believe in filming *The Crowd* (1928) I was one of the
first directors to journey from California to New York to
shoot scenes with actors working on city streets and to use
the normal flow of pedestrians and traffic for atmosphere.
Most of the scenes were photographed through a hole cut
in the rear curtain of a delivery truck which we parked at
an advantageous point at the curb. The brief rehearsals
were all worked out by myself and two assistants, one of
whom dressed in the costume favored by truck drivers and
leaned against the tail gate of the truck in order to relay
messages inconspicuously inside. Arm signals prevailed.
In about ten days of shooting we employed no extras for
the street scenes, nor do I recall that anyone detected what
was happening.

For some perambulating walking shots we constructed
what appeared to be three packing boxes mounted on a
rubber-tired push cart but inside we hid a camera operator
with his tripod-mounted camera.

Two summers ago I visited the Yugoslav city of Zagreb
as guest of Jadran Films, the most important and best
equipped production organization in the country. I had
heard that the film *Fiddler on the Roof* was being made
in and around Zagreb using Jadran Studios as their base of
operations. The producer-director of the film, Norman
Jewison, was a friend of mine and I looked forward to a
visit to the shooting set.

The first morning I came down into the lobby of the
Intercontinental Hotel where I was staying, I was sur-

prised to see several pages of a typical English-American movie call sheet prominently displayed on one of the lobby's structural columns. I read each item with a great deal of interest. I had been in Venice for two weeks after which I had taken a weeks' cruise on the Adriatic with stops at such fascinating places as Dubrovnik and Split, but the words *wrangler, gaffer, grip,* and *honey wagon* quickly transported me across two continents and a wide ocean to a place called Hollywood.

Whenever horses are required in a scene you must have a *wrangler* with you. All the other members of the crew might go blank when it comes to controlling live stock in a scene but with a wrangler along the director simply tells his assistant, the assistant tells the wrangler and the wrangler, in no uncertain terms tells the horses, and they do it.

A *gaffer* is the chief electrician. Those gaffers who work with the same cinematographer over a period of years through a long list of films become so well versed in lighting techniques followed by the photographer that they can expertly light the set and the scene.

A *grip* is a sort of specialized carpenter-handyman. The *chief grip* stays close to the camera at all times. He lays the track for perambulating and moving boom shots. He shields the camera from intruding light beams that can produce glare in the lens and takes care of a thousand and one last minutes chores that are impossible to anticipate in the film's scheduling. I believe the name came from the vernacular of the theater. A grip was the fellow who secured the flats of scenery to the stage floor using long wooden braces with metal ends. A wide-handled screw was used to grip these braces to the scenery and to the stage.

I wish I could tell you where the word *honey wagon* originated. A honey wagon is a trailer or self-propelled truck equipped with four to six chemical toilets. In some instances I have even heard of a private throne for the

45......DAY OF SHOOTING | MIRISCH PRODS. INC. & JADRAN FILM | DAY: FRIDAY,

SHOOTING CALL

DATE: 2nd OCTOBER, 197

Pict. No. 7001   "FIDDLER ON THE ROOF"   Producer/Director: NORMAN JEWISON

SHOOTING CALL: 6.00pm   CREW CALL: 4.00pm   (Except as noted)   Associate Producer: PATRICK PALMER

(1) EXT. SYNAGOGUE: Scs.203,204,212,213 pt. Night for Night. MALA GORICA
(2) EXT. INN: Scs.127, 128. Night for Night - MALA GORICA
(3) EXT. LAZAR WOLF'S: Sc.120 - Night for Night - MALA GORICA
(4) WEATHER COVER: INT. TEVYE'S HOUSE, SLEEPING LOFT: Scs. 62, 63, 64, 65, 66pt. Day. DOME STAGE, MALA GORIC

ARTIST	CHARACTER	LEAVE HOTEL p.m.	HAIRDRESSING	MAKE-UP p.m.	READY ON SET p.m.
Topol	Tevye	3.45		4.45	6.00
Norma Crane	Golde	3.50		4.45	6.00
Rosalind Harris	Tzeitel	3.45		4.45	6.00
Michele Marsh	Hodel	4.15		5.15	6.00
Neva Small	Chava	4.15		5.15	6.00
Elaine Edwards	Shprintze	4.45		5.45	6.00
Candy Bonstein	Bielke	4.45		5.45	6.00
Molly Picon	Yente	3.45		4.45	6.00
Leonard Frey	Motel	4.15		5.15	6.00
Michael Glaser	Perchik	4.15		5.15	6.00
Paul Mann	Lazar Wolf	4.15		5.15	6.00
Shimen Ruskin	Mordcha	4.15		5.15	6.00
Zvee Scooler	Rabbi	4.15		5.15	6.00
Barry Dennen	Mendel	4.15		5.15	6.00
Alfie Scopp	Avram	4.15		5.15	6.00
Howard Goorney	Nachum	4.15		5.15	6.00
Louis Zorich	Constable	Hold			
Raymond Lovelock	Fyedk	Hold			
Stella Courtney	Shandel	4.15		5.15	6.00
Tutte Lemkow	Fiddler	4.15		5.15	6.00

DAY PLAYERS—ATMOSPHERE—STANDINS	PICKUP	WARDROBE	MAKEUP	READY ON SET
PHOTO DOUBLE FOR TEVYE: EXTRAS FOR: LAZAR WOLF, FIDDLER MOTEL, GOLDE, TZEITEL, HODEL, CHAVA SHPRINTZE, BIELKE.	3.30 p.m. leave Zagreb			6.00 p.m.
ATMOSPHERE: 30 JEWISH ME., 30 JEWISH WOMEN 20 JEWISH BOYS, 20 JEWISH GIRLS SOSSIE'S 2 GIRLS GNESSI BOY & GIRL HONE'S 2 SONS: DEAL'S 2 SONS	3.30 p.m. leave Zagreb 4.30 p.m. Wardrobe Mala Gorica			6.00 p.m.
8 STUNTMEN	Leave Zagreb 4.00 p.m.			

ADVANCE SCHEDULE

SATURDAY, 3rd OCTOBER: EXT. SHTETL MARKET PLACE Scs. 218, 219, 221, 233A. Night

SUNDAY, 4th OCTOBER. R E S T D A Y.

T. NELSON—P. IBBETSON
Asst. Directors

B. LUSTIG
Prod. Mgr. (Jadran)

L. DE WAAY
Prod. Supervisor

TRANSPORTATION REQUIREMENTS

LOCATION: MALA GORICA

DATE: FRIDAY, 2nd OCTOBER, 1970

VEHICLE	FROM	TIME
Car 1 D.Mann		
1 N.Jewison		13.30
2		
3		
4		
Car 2 D.Melnick		
1 Topol		15.45
2		
3		
4		
Car 3 Merc		
1 P.Mann	Esp.	16.15
2 A.Scopp	"	"
3 Z.Scooler	"	"
4		
Car 4 Milan		
1 Office		6.30
2		
3 G.Offenheim	Int.	14.45
4		
Car 5		
1 H.Grigsby	Int.	15.30
2 M.Picon	Esp.	15.45
3 R.Morris	"	"
4 N.Crane	Int.	15.50
Car 6		
1 Branko	O	C
2		
3		
4		
Car 7		
1 Buco	O	C
2		
3		
4		
Car 8		
1 B.Maldonado	O	C
2 V.Despotovic		
3		
4		
Car 9		
1 B.Boyle	Int.	13.45
2		
3		
4		
Car 10		
1 P.Palmer	O	C
2		
3 Car 11:		
4 L.De Waay	O	C
Mini-Bus 12		
1 T.Nelson Illcs		13.30
2 O.Morris	Int.	13.45
3 J.Purrell	"	"
4 E.Schreyeck	"	"
5 D.Hildyard	"	"
6 M.Arnold	"	"
7 D.Fraser	"	"
Mini-Bus 13 S/by	Int.	15.00
1 Yugo Ward.	Int.	15.30
2 Seka	"	"
3 Yugo H/Up	"	"
4 Yugo Hair	"	"
5		
6 Vehicle 44	M.G.	17.00
7 (Jeep)		

VEHICLE	FROM	TIME
Mini-Bus 14	Int.	13.45
1 D.Armstrong	"	13.45
2 V.Schneiderman	"	15.30
3 Gordon Boud	"	"
4 E.Fletcher	"	"
5 C.Jamison	"	"
6 M.Morris	"	"
7 J.Jamison	"	"
8		
Mini-Bus 15 S/by	Int.	15.00
1 E.Edwards	Int.	16.45
2 C.Bonstein	"	"
3 J.Sharpe	"	"
4 Mrs.Bonstein	"	"
5 Susan Twigg	"	"
6		
7		
8		
Mini-Bus 16		
1 D.Carruth	Int.	13.40
2 L.Carruth	"	"
3 T.Abbott	Esp.	13.45
4 S.Bayes	"	"
5		
6 Car 34:		
7 J.Stears	Int.	16.00
8 J.Fitt,S.Wyatt	"	"
Mini-Bus 17		
1 J.Cummins	Int.	15.30
2 D.Edwards	"	"
3 J.Dodson	"	"
4 J.Hilling	"	"
5 D.Murphy	"	"
6 B.Knight	"	"
7		
8		
Mini-Bus 18		
1 P.Lamont	Int.	16.00
2 M.Lennon	"	"
3 M.Weymouth	"	"
4 Gljiva	"	"
5 Stanislav	"	"
6 Sam Gordon	Zap.	16.05
7		
8		
Bus 1 9		
Jim Bray	Int.	16.00
Jack Newman	"	"
Joe Finn	"	"
Bill Morgen	"	"
Yugo Stagehands	"	"
Yugo Electr.	"	"
Truck Drivers	"	"
Nurse	"	"
8 Stuntmen	"	"
Jeep Driver	"	"
Minibus 37:		
Leonard Frey	Esp.	16.15
H.Glaser	"	"
M.Marsh	"	"
Nevs Small	"	"
J.Ruskin	"	"
Tutte Lemkov	"	"
Zharon Ipale	"	"

VEHICLE	FROM	TIME
Bus 2 0	Int.	16.10
A.Haverstock	C.Bass	
L.Winter	L.Wright	
C.Bilham	H.Krein	Esp. 16.15
H.Grigsby	H.Lewis	
H.Goorney	B.Fleet	
S.Courtney	H.Wright	
O.Diamant	C.Jaffe	
B.Dennen	M.Malicz	
D.Grumber	A.Diamond	
B.Coburn	.Iverie	
M.Rivera	H.Kriseman	
G.Little	S.Cohen	
H.Ditson	J.Harte	
S.Sloman	K.Robson	
J.Rudnick	R.Durbin	
L.Zemprogna	B.Stevensen	
Minibus 43:	Int.	15.00
L.Crowe	Int.	16.00
J.Higgins	"	"
F.Richardson	"	"
Bill Hughes	"	"
Bert Hughes	"	"
Car 38:		
E.Haffenden	Esp.	13.45
J.Bridge	"	"
Addl. Buses and Cars		
1 Car 39 (Publicity)		
2 W.Donoghue	Esp.	15.55
3 D.James	"	16.00
4		
Minibus 40:		
5 Editorial	O	C
2 Extras buses	Zagreb	15
Camera Truck T.V.	Int.	15.30
Sound Truck	"	15.45
Titan Crane	Mala Gorica	
Electric Truck	"	"
Prop-Dressing Truck	"	"
Grip S.E. Truck	"	"
Wardrobe Van	Int.	15.30
Generator	Mala Gorica	
Catering Truck	"	"
Catering Land-Rover	"	"
Honeywagon		
Honeywagon-Extras		
Utility Truck		
Generator	C Lekenik	
* Incl.horse trailer		
Grip Gorice/Lekenik		
Utility "	"	

MISCELLANEOUS REQUIREMENTS

	FROM	TIME
Lunches		
Dinners (225)	From	8.00p
Car 42:		
V.Spindler	Esp.	15.00
T.Churcher	"	"
L.Ibbetson	Int.	15.05
Minibus 44: Extra/	O	C
Casting		

PRODUCTION REQUIREMENTS

DIRECTOR: NORMAN JEWISON **Pict. No. 7001**

DATE: FRIDAY, 2nd OCT., 1970

CAMERA	FROM	TIME	STAFF	FROM	TIME	JADRAN STAFF and CREW	FROM	TIME
Cameraman	Int.	13.45	Asst. to Producer	London				
Operator	"	"	Production Designer	Int.	13.45	Prod. Manager	0	C
Focus	"	"	Art Director	London		Asst. Prod. Manager	0	C
Clapper-Loader	Int.	15.30	Const. Co-ordinator	0	C	Prod. Organizar 1		
Stillman	"	16.00	Continuity	Int.	13.45	Prod. Organizer 2	Int.	15.30
			Prod. Secretary	"	14.45	Prod. Organizer 3	"	"
			Prod. Accountant	0	C	Prod. Secretary 1	Off.	6.30
			Location Auditor	0	C	Prod. Secretary 2	"	11.00
SOUND			* Film Editors (2)	Int.	8.00	Publicity Secretary	"	9.00
Mixer	Int.	13.45	Asst. Film Editors (3)	"	"	Accountant	"	8.00
Maintenance	"	15.45	Technical Advisor			Cashier	"	8.00
Boom-man	"	"	Tutor	Int.	16.45	Office interpreter	"	8.00
Playback Operator	"	"	Publicist	Esp.	15.55	Stagehand 1	Int.	16.00
						Stagehand 2	"	"
						Stagehand 3	"	"
ELECTRICAL						Propman 1	"	"
Gaffer	Int.	16.00	WARDROBE			Propman 2	"	"
Chargehand	"	"	Costume Designers (2)	Esp.	13.45	Propman 3	0	C
Lamp Operator	"	"	Wardrobe Supervisor	Int.	15.30	Wardrobe 1	Int.	15.30
Generator Operator	"	"	Wardrobe Woman (3)	"	"	Wardrobe 2	"	"
			Wardrobe Man	"	"	Wardrobe 3	"	"
			Wardrobe Man	"	"	Wardrobe 4	"	"
TECHNICAL						Makeup	"	"
Grip	Int.	16.00				Makeup		
Rigger	"	"	MAKEUP			Hairdressers	Int.	15.30
Stage Hand	"	"	Key Makeup Artists 1	Int.	13.45	Hairdressers	"	"
Carpenter	"	"	Makeup Artist 1	Int.	15.30	Interpreter 1	Int.	16.00
Crane Operator	"	"	Makeup Artist	"	"	Interpreter 2	"	15.30
Crane Grip			Hairdresser	"	"	Electricians (4)	"	16.00
			Hairdresser	"	"	Electricians (6)	"	16.00
Special Effects	"	"				Construction		
Special Effects						Construction		
(1) Wet down			MUSIC			Nurse	Int.	16.00
(2) Smoke Effects			Musical Director	---		Casting	0	C
(3) Fire & flame effects			Music Consultant			Laborers Set 4 Lekenik	7.30	
Painter	Int.	16.00	Rehearsal Pianist	Int.	13.40	Laborers		
				---		Head Wrangler (1) Mala Gorica		
PROPERTY			Music for: "Rich Man" Fiddler			Wranglers (1)	"	"
Propmaster	Zep.	16.05	Theme: PB 19			Wranglers		
Set Decorator	"	16.00	"To Life": PB 13			Watchmen (10)	0	C
Prop Dresser	"	"	"Sunrise, Sunset": PB 5A			Policemen		
Propman	"	"	DANCE "Matchmaker": PB 1			Firemen		
			Choreographer	Esp.	13.45	2 add. Hairdr.	Int.	15.30
Vehicles			Asst. Choreographer	"	"			
2 caravans Mala Gorica			* Moviola to be on Dome Stage					
			with "Matchmaker" film for					
			Scenes 62 - 66 pt. (Day).					
Livestock								
7 Horses (for Russian								
Riders)								
4.00 p.m. Mala Gorica								

ARTIST	CHARACTER	LEAVE HOTEL p.m.	HAIRDRESSING	MAKE-UP p.m.	READY ON SET p.m.
Otto Diamont	Yussel	4.15		5.15	6.00
Aharon Ipale	Sheftel	"		"	"
Dorothy Grumbar	Sossie	"		"	"
Brian Coburn	Berl	"		"	"
Marika Riviera	Rifka	"		"	"
George Little	Hone	"		"	"
Judith Harte	Gnessi	"		"	"
Harry Ditson	Leibosh	"		"	"
Joel Rudnick	Marcus	"		"	"
Michael Lewis	Joshua	"		"	"
Stanley Fleet	Farcel	"		"	"
Hazel Wright	Rebecca	"		"	"
Carl Jaffe	Isaac	"		"	"
Mark Malicz	Ezekial	"		"	"
Arnold Diamond	Moishe	"		"	"
Miki Iverla	Bess	"		"	"
Hilda Kriseman	Zelda	"		"	"
Sarah Cohen	Bashe	"		"	"
Susan Sloman	Nechama	"		"	"
Larry Bianco	Igor				
Jody Hall	Jewish Dancer	Hold			
Ivan Baptie	" "	"			
Michael Ingleton	" "	"			
Barry Lines	" "	"			
Ken Robson	" "	4.15		5.15	6.00
Adam Scott	" "	Hold			
Bob Stevenson	" "	4.15		5.15	6.00
Lou Zamprogna	" "	"		"	"
Roy Durbin	" "	"		"	"
Albin Pahernik	" "	Hold			
Pippa Reynaud	" "	"			
Karen Trent	" "	"			
Inc Claire	" "	"			
Tanya Bayona	" "	"			
A. Haverstock	Violinist	4.10		5.15	6.00
C. Bass	Drummer	"		"	"
M. Winter	Clarinetist	"		"	"
L. Wright	Trumpeter	"		"	"
C. Bilham	Bassist	"		"	"
H. Krein	Accordionist	"		"	"

male and female stars—a most useful addition to any first-
class production unit. Imagine my surprise when I encountered my friend the honey wagon in far off Zagreb.
Once again, the exigencies of artistic communication overcome all political boundaries.

I notice in examining the transportation requirements
more closely that there is need of a second honey wagon
for the extras and besides a camera truck, a sound truck,
orders are in for a titan crane, an electric truck, a prop-
dressing truck, a grip special-effects truck, a wardrobe van,
a generator, a catering truck, a catering land-rover (whatever that is), a utility truck, and a horse trailer.

Dinners are ordered for two hundred twenty-five persons
among whom are eight stunt men and a nurse (an understandable precaution), a choreographer with an assistant, a
music consultant, a production designer, a construction
coordinator, a continuity girl, a production secretary, a
production accountant, a location auditor, two film editors
with three assistants, a technical advisor, a tutor and a pub-
licist. Do you get an inkling of why picture costs run
into the millions? Why it probably cost five thousand
dollars for the director to pay a visit to the number one
honey wagon?

There is one story out of Hollywood that concerns a
quickie company whose schedule was so tight they didn't
know whether they would have time to let their star go to
the toilet. Finally the director said, "Let him go. We'll
shoot around him until he gets back." "Shoot around" in
Hollywood verbage means to take some scenes, close-ups
perhaps, in which the star does not appear.

On the Yugoslavian call sheets the company assistants
seem to have left off no one who could possibly be needed
on a big musical production such as *Fiddler*. I have recently come across in a University Cinema Department call
sheet a contributor the *Fiddler* assistant probably over-

looked. He is called a *gopher,* namely, the little guy who goes for things.

The multiplication of men and machines behind the camera made it increasingly difficult for the director to retain his individual viewpoint. When Joseph Von Sternberg worked as one of my assistants on *Duel in the Sun,* he told me he didn't understand how I kept my cool with all the apparent confusion taking place around our set. That's just it; the confusion was only apparent, not actual. I have learned in my life to examine each quick judgment before accepting the other fellow's viewpoint. To Von Sternberg, it appeared to be confusion; in my opinion, everything going on had a purpose.

In the noise and hullabaloo of a busy set, I have often had to close my eyes and my mind, and remember back to a quieter moment, generally when I was concentrating on the scene during the writing of the screenplay. This quieter and more concentrated concept has often proved to be my salvation. I would then hold to this earlier concept in spite of all the pressures of the moment. The definite resolve cut through all obstacles.

Today there is a tendency to return to the earlier methods of simplicity. Some directors, who have been trained to operate cameras and lighting, are photographing their own pictures. One of the most notable examples of this double roll is the French film *A Man and a Woman.* For years, more orthodox cameramen went to elaborate means to block out reflections in an automobile windshield; but Claude LeLouch made a beautiful asset out of the moving reflections of the tree branches along a country road in France, and every cinematographer filming a moving automobile scene has been trying to imitate him ever since.

The recent proliferation of craftsmen and technicians for operating, coordinating, and controlling an increasingly sophisticated film technology makes it imperative for the film maker to always keep in mind my earlier point: a movie is an optical illusion and the film maker is the chief illusionist. This awareness will free him and his imagination and impress him with the conviction that he must always control the medium rather than the reverse. This attitude is not a rejection of realism as it first may seem. Since I thoroughly believe in the subjective "I" as beholder and creator, I am perfectly agreeable to using an illusory device as a medium of expression. It has been said that beauty is in the eye of the beholder. In contrast, Marshall McLuhan states "the medium is the message." Somewhere in between the two but encompassing both statements you will find what I am talking about. All action in daily experience is said to be no more than a series of still images or impressions blurred together into action. So we discover that the so-called illusion of cinematographic projection is no more than a mechanized analysis of how we actually see the world. Thus, the distinction between the "illusion" of film and the "facts" of our daily existence is a superficial one; on a deeper level the two terms are equal and interchangeable.

In short, on a large production set every technician is making a valid contribution. But if there is to be any coherence about the final scene he must follow the unifying conception of one man. That man is, and must be, the director.

CHAPTER 2

THE DIRECTOR

■

In pointing out that film is a director's medium I am not saying that the author of the story, the writer of the screenplay, the actors, the photographers, the sound recording crew do not all make valuable contributions, but they all like to know precisely what the director has in mind. Each member of the crew is unhappy when working with a director who doesn't know what he wants. We come back to first principles. If your approach to film making is that of a director, when you go into a working set, you should have prepared yourself by first laying out in your own mind exactly the way the scene is to be made; the next step is to let every fellow working with you know as much about your concept as you can. They will appreciate it.

Someone else may be controlling the purse strings of the budget, he may even designate what actors you can use. The author of the original story may never have heard of you when he wrote his book, stage play, or screenplay. The leading players may have well established reputations as screen personalities before they agreed to make this picture; but when they go on the stage they are under your control and what goes through the lens and is registered onto film is in your responsibility to approve, to reject, to mold, to create.

If the director is worth talking about here, he should have been formulating his work long before he went onto

the stage to begin photography. If he didn't have the opportunity to work with the author on the original story, he
should have had a close relationship with the writer of the
screenplay. Many directors write their own screenplays but
if a director feels that a better result will be achieved by a
close collaboration with a writer, this should be his choice.
Often I have found an advantage in the collaborative
method in that it enables me, the director, to preserve an
objectivity that I might not be able to maintain if I chose
to tackle the job alone. Also I might well be a more severe
task-master with someone else than I would be with myself. This decision of whether to write the screenplay yourself or to work in collaboration must be a choice made
by the individual while taking into account the particular
circumstances surrounding the film. But as far as I am
concerned, except in the rarest of conditions, the writer
of the final screenplay should never work entirely apart
from the director.

A recent example of this was with a producer with
whom I had made an arrangement to make a film from a
book we both thought had good possibilities. He was a
second-generation movie producer and I had had the same
problems with his father who thought the director and the
script writer should be kept far apart. I suppose this particular blindness of vision had been inherited by the son.
With the films I had made for the father I had managed to
circumvent his rigid concept by working clandestinely
with the writer who in each case welcomed the collaboration. In these instances I would forego any official screen
credit. But the son managed to enforce such an isolation
between writer and director that I was finally forced to
accept the situation. Fortunately, my attorney had written
into the working arrangement a clause stating that if I
didn't approve the final script I would not have to make
the film.

Three complete scripts were written—each of which I rejected. Final result, I withdrew from the project and the film was abandoned. In trying to evaluate what has happened to Hollywood we can chalk up the lack of perception just illustrated as one of the reasons for its demise. In the course of my long career I have read only two completed screenplays which I would have willingly gone on the set to shoot without any major change. I think there is a lesson here and it has to do with the director as an individual.

The foregoing sorry example can be applied to every other contributor in making a film. Be prepared to tell each one of them what you want. This is not a question of egoism but of unity which is another way of saying artistic achievement.

To cite an incident that made a lasting impression on me. At the M.G.M. studio Margaret Rawlins' well-known book *The Yearling* was being readied for a production Victor Fleming was to direct. A conference was held in the office of Cedric Gibbons, head of the art department, which included Fleming and the unit art director assigned to the film. The meeting lasted all day at the end of which Gibbons asked Fleming what he thought had been accomplished. Fleming, replying in his usual dour, taciturn manner said, "Nothing."

Gibbons, rather shocked, said, "Well, *you* contributed nothing all day."

Now it was Fleming's turn to be surprised. "What do you mean I contributed nothing, didn't I say 'No' all day?"

I believe one has to understand the workings of a large studio to get the full impact of Fleming's meaning.

The director's domain is broad in scope. After two months of photography on location in Florida on the same film, Fleming and Spencer Tracy, who was playing one of the star parts, had a disagreement and both flew back to the studio demanding to be taken off the picture. All production was suspended. After a week's layoff when it was certain that their differences could not be amicably resolved, I was called in to take over the direction of the film.

The first morning of my chore when I was just beginning to look at the film shot to date I received a telephone call from an employee on the Florida location.

"We have forty thousand cans of growing corn down here. What shall we do with them?"

I knew by now that a corn field of varying maturity for subsequent episodes played a major part in the story, but my unfamiliarity with all the details of the production left me only one reply.

"Water them!" I said and hung up.

I was in charge of the picture for only a few weeks when the studio had to suspend further production until spring of the following year. The following is the almost unbelievable reason.

Jody, the young boy in the story, had captured and made a pet out of a small fawn. The time span of the entire story was only a few weeks—a short period, to say the least. During the shooting of the film, which spread over several months, the little fawn would grow up. It seems that young deer mature rapidly. A very young fawn had to be available for each day's shooting. Therefore, a production line of pregnant does was set up both on the Florida location and on one of the back lots in Culver City. Breeding had to be controlled so that all fawns would not be born at the same time. But—and this *but* cost the company close to a million dollars—it was not natural for a doe to produce offspring after a certain month each year.

Oblivious to the screams of top studio executives the fawn production line suddenly came to a halt. The does refused, even for M.G.M., to change the course of nature.

The following year when production of the picture was

resumed Gregory Peck had been substituted for Spencer Tracy and Clarence Brown had assumed the direction. By then I was off in the wilds of Idaho directing *Northwest Passage*.

The film director must be able to answer any question relating to any part of the production. In contrast to the stage director he must be able to shoot a scene from any part of the film at any time. For obvious economical reasons the scenes are not photographed in chronological order but in any way (backward, jumbled, or by location) that works best on a production manager's schedule board. In the theater the actors go through their parts from beginning to end all in a few hours. With film, the scenes are shot over a period of weeks and months. A film director must be aware of each fragment and make certain that in the final editing it will all fit together harmoniously.

The film director must be a writer, a dramatist, a painter, an editor, a technician, and a musician. He must be thoroughly familiar with photography, budgeting, and acting. He must be artist and executive at the same time and must be able to work early and late for long periods. If he has some training in architecture and knows something about period costumes and women's clothes and make-up this will be a great help to him; if he went to military school or served a stretch in the army or navy, this experience will be useful when staging a battle scene.

In view of the world-wide nature of movie production today a pretty fair knowledge of French, Italian, and Spanish will come in handy. And last but not least, if he gets stuck with a couple of neurotic actors in his cast some training in psychology wouldn't be amiss. With all these accomplishments as prerequisites is it any wonder that so many students in high school and college have singled out movie directing as an exciting career.

Even after he has nursed the picture through the labora-

tory, the editing room, and had his say with the composer
of the musical score the director might well be asked to
make a tour of major cities in the United States and
Europe to sell his film to the public. He can't refuse—it is
his baby. He has to wet nurse it until it is out of its
swaddling clothes and able to stand on its own.

The director as a writer: If he cannot find a story that
suits him, he must be able to write his own.

As a dramatist: If the adapter of the original material,
the writer of the screenplay, is faulty in his task, the film
maker should be able to write his own. At the very least he
must be able to guide the writer to show him the form he
wants to follow. He will have little authority if he is unable to show those with whom he works how the job
should be done.

As a painter: In color photography his work will be
directly affected by the color he uses. He must know the
dramatic value of all the colors. In the film *Blow-Up,*
Antonioni repainted whole blocks of houses to create a
mood. The buildings he painted were only used as background for a traveling shot. Colors of clothes, of interior
walls, of furniture, of skies can all contribute or detract
from the desired dramatic effect. In one of my films a light
blue sky would have softened the sombre effect I wanted.
I moved the exterior scene onto a stage and had a backing
painted a color in keeping with the scene.

As an editor: After he has shot miles of film in the rush
and excitement he must be able to go into the editing
room with objective standards foremost in his mind and
cut each sequence to its optimum length. Proper editing is
so essential, so integral to directing that the Director's
Guild has long made it obligatory for the director to
supervise the first cut of his film.

As a technician: Making a film is an exercise in inven-
tiveness and in overcoming technical mishaps. The direc-

tor, if he is mechanically-minded, can take the lead in solving many of these problems. Tricks, illusions, and gadgets are all necessary in the daily routine.

As a photographer: The more a director knows about photography the better off he is. Fifty-mm, 40mm tele-photo and zoom lenses as well as filters, film speeds, pan, and perambulating shots must be part of his vocabulary and he should be familiar with their uses. I will go into more detail on this in a later chapter.

As an actor: Suppose an actor says, "How would you read this line?" or "Show me what you mean?" What are you going to do if you don't know something about acting?

You cannot ignore these facets of a director's responsi-bilities during the making of a film. You will be chal-lenged on every one of them and more. Contrary to popu-lar belief, the director's job doesn't consist of telling actors where to stand, when to sit down, when to move. This is how you might have felt when you directed your first high school play, but it is only the beginning

For the first days work on a film I try to schedule some scenes that are not too difficult on either the actors or the director. I will have worked out beforehand the general movement but I will not adhere to this so rigidly that it will prevent the actors from feeling free to move as they feel; nor will I allow it to become so frozen in my mind that it will stifle a sense of improvisation. For me it is a pattern on which to base a beginning. In some instances I decide to let the movement grow out of the actors' first rehearsal. The pattern they establish then becomes a blue-print for the cinematographer and chief electrician.

The last half-hour of each shooting day is given over to rehearsals for the scenes to be shot on the next. If the set is available, I have one or two walk-throughs for the purpose of giving the actors time to think about what they will do the next morning. This practice is also a great help to the photographer as it enables him to get started an hour before the cast arrives in the morning: by using stand-ins for members of the cast he will be able to have the lights rigged in advance.

As the cast moves through the rehearsals, the photographer is moving with them, watching through his finder. The director can observe the camera positions out of the corner of his eye. If there is a variance of opinion, the director can indicate his choice with a hand motion without disturbing the dialogue being spoken by the actors. Each cast rehearsal, in addition to benefiting the performances, also serves to clarify the positioning of the camera, the lights, and the microphone.

The director must be careful not to over-rehearse. Too many rehearsals can deplete the spontaneity of the performances. I try to anticipate when a peak performance will next occur and make certain the camera and sound will be rolling.

On the set, don't be nervous about assuming command. I cannot overemphasize the fact that your co-workers want and look for a definite viewpoint. The best way that I know of to fortify yourself against doubt is to be more familiar with the story and the screenplay than anyone else. This is not difficult: it is a safe bet that no one else on the set has worked on the script and the preliminary planning. Remember, the film will be slanted from your viewpoint and certainly no one is more qualified to give answers than you.

The thought has occurred to me many times that most films are good in the pre-production discussions. Nobody starts out to make a bad film. In a large percentage of the cases, something happens along the way to spoil the goal. What is it?

First, I would say, is the inability to bring to screen-life those thoughts and ideas that were discussed so painstakingly in the conferences; in other words, the inability to succeed in visual interpretation; the confusion brought about by the pressures of time and money, schedules and budgets. But the ability to shoot fast and decisively under any circumstances should be part of the film maker's craft.

Then too, when several important members of the cast are going through their parts in a capable but uninspired way (what is sometimes referred to as "being there in body only") the performances suffer. On the screen, actors can't cheat or fake as they can on the stage. The tremendous enlargement of image and voice is a dead give-away. You might as well try to fool your psychoanalyst. Actors must bring as much of their own individuality to the part as the part brings to them: it is a two-way street. (See photos 8 and 9.)

I think the underlying reason for mediocrity in film is the avoidance of clarity, the fear to say what you mean, or, to put it bluntly, the lack of anything to say in the first place. This is almost a universal trait and accounts for the great interest in "subtlety." The director, as an artist, cannot afford to skirt central issues. He cannot follow the example of those people who are afraid to talk about sex and so express themselves through dirty jokes; or who don't want to tackle philosophical subjects and expend their mental energy on abstract gamesmanship instead.

As you cannot go along and give an explanation with every showing of your film, I heartily recommend that, in spite of a few successful examples to the contrary, you let your film voice speak with clarity and definition. Don't hide behind a curtain of abstraction.

I wont go over again all the things you were taught in film school such as where to put the lights, what speed film to use, whether to take a close-up, medium shot or long shot. Each film is a different challenge and carries along with it most of the answers to purely technical problems.

Be inventive and ingenious and never let anyone tell you that what you want cannot be done. A good answer to that one is, "Yes I know, but I'm going to do it anyhow."

During the shooting of *Duel in the Sun* in Tucson, Arizona, I returned to the hotel one evening to be greeted in the lobby by the producer of the film, David O. Selznick. Mr. Selznick was also the writer of the screenplay. The night before we had been discussing the preparation for some difficult sequence of scenes.

Selznick said, "Come up to my room, I want to see if I can talk you into a compromise on that sequence."

I was too exhausted from a long day in the sun to indulge in polite conversation. I said, "I am not against compromise, David, as long as I can do the scene the way I want to."

David laughed very hard but I hadn't tried consciously to be funny. There was no more talk about compromise.

A number of film makers have written their autobiographies. In their books, they have told *what* they did and about the obstacles they surmounted to accomplish what they did. But they have not told *how* they made the films that made them successful and famous. I doubt if very many of them could. It has been said of writing that it is an act of faith. Film directing is an act of faith—and love. I am tempted to say that one should not become analytical where faith is concerned. While this may be true of love, when faith is first analyzed and then embraced it becomes understanding, while unexamined faith can be blind dogmatism. True understanding is an enrichment of the individual psyche or soul.

Frank Capra in his autobiography, *The Name Above the Title,* says that at one point in his career he made the following decision about the content of his future films:

"I would sing the songs of the working stiffs, of the

short-changed Joes, the born poor, the afflicted. I would gamble with the long-shot players who light candles in the wind, and resent with the pushed-around because of race or birth. Above all, I would fight for their causes on the screens of the world."

The decision was evidently a good one: the next three or four films that he made were among his best. But this rather vague generalization is about as articulate as he can become about his work. One must look to the man himself. The determined upward struggle out of the confines of a poor imigrant family, the Horatio Alger glory of success. Capra, the winner of Academy Awards in contrast to the little Italian newspaper boy, is what makes these films what they are; Capra, in his victory, was putting his own story, his own hopes, on the screen.

What can I say to you from one film maker to another? Shall I instruct you to be born into an Italian immigrant family with the fears and frustrations engendered by their arrival in a strange and broad land? No. It is too late for that. You must be ready to go as you are.

But I can ask, "Who are you?" You should not be quick to answer for there may be a story in your reply. Maybe a whole series of stories as happened to Capra. Take your time and when you feel you have gotten hold of somebody —yourself—go in, not as an amateur, but as a professional.

CHAPTER 3

THE ACTOR AND HOW
TO CAST HIM

$\boxed{\bullet}$

I made most of my films in an era when big-name stars reigned supreme. Stars were made principally by appearing in a series of films in which they played more or less the same character. In most instances they were simply playing themselves rather than creating a new role based on some character delineated by the screen play. This soon led to the star becoming a symbol rather than developing into an actor capable of a virtuoso performance. While I readily acknowledge that Bette Davis was considered a great actress and Spencer Tracy a great actor, the sparseness of those so labeled only goes to prove my point.

It took me years to learn that the big stars had established symbols that shouldn't be tampered with. A director could consider himself fortunate if the principal character in his screen play was identical to the character symbolized by one of the available stars. But whatever situation he found himself in, it was a mistake to try to reshape the character symbolized by the star to fit a different character called for in the screenplay.

In one of my films, *American Romance,* the leading character fitted Spencer Tracy perfectly. I had him in mind all the time I was working on the story and script. When I gave him the screenplay to read he seemed in-

terested but a few days later I heard he was going to do
another film. I went to him and asked what had happened. He said if I could wait he would do my film immediately after the film he had chosen to do first. I thought
the part in my film was much greater than the one he had
chosen and I couldn't understand his decision. My emotional reaction went as follows:

The project and part is so tremendous that I am not dependent on Mr. Tracy. I can find someone else just as good
and then I will make him regret that he chose another film
over mine. Yes, after many years and a long list of successful films, I was this immature emotionally. And just at this
time I was called in by the top executives of M.G.M. and
asked to look at a film starring an actor they hoped to develop into a big-name-star.

Brian Donlevy was a splendid actor in his way but how
far does acting go if his screen personality is different from
the one needed to fulfill the goal of the project?

Previously Donlevy had effectively played the role of a
corrupt politician. This may have had some effect on his
ability to become a symbol of heroism and determination,
while the personality he projected had resolution, with the
tremendous enlargement of the cinema screen the viewer
felt in him a strain of uncertainty, of insecurity. I have
seen the film recently after the passage of time has removed
all speculation as to exigencies of its various parts. Donlevy
gives a fine performance but as a star he does not symbolize
that intangible element that would have lifted the role
to greatness.

Tracy as a man had many personal and emotional problems but that is not what came through on the screen. This
is a paradox I won't attempt to explain here. Perhaps the
answer is one of successful compensation. I do know that
actors who have some sort of emotional problem going on

underneath seem to give a more interesting performance on top.

Practically all feminine stars in the history of films have at one time or another wanted to play a prostitute. But let one of them who had risen to fame symbolizing purity and romance try it: the shattering reaction of audiences, robbed of their beloved symbol of innocence, would have been felt around the world. This explains why a director often wants to cast unestablished or unlabeled performers as his leads. The roles as written or developed will carry more conviction; the established symbol will not stand in the way.

But don't misunderstand me. The chosen actors must have something to bring to the part in order to make the film click. What process does a director use to detect this value? The usual one is a screen test but these are not infallible. I have on two occasions had actors make such a determined effort to get the part through the making of a test that they were never able to equal their performance when the film was in production.

In silent film days I used to ask that prospective actors bring in at least a dozen still photographs from the roles they had played. If all photographs showed only one mood or expression, I would continue my search.

In more recent years I have kept the following thought in mind while interviewing for parts in a film: "Giving an actor a role requires something in return. We have worked for months, maybe years, to bring this role into being. If we give the role to you, what are you going to bring to the film? I think the deal should at least be on a fifty-fifty basis."

These are not my words but they give a pattern to my decision. I am not thinking of money but of contributions to the finished product. Some performers are there in body

only and only do what they are told. Others bring an
added, indefinable dimension to their part. The director
can explain until he is blue in the face. He can beg, plead,
and wheedle but he can only go so far. An actor either has
it, or he hasn't.

Whenever for some reason or other I have appeared
before the camera instead of *behind* it, I have suddenly become aware of the two directly opposite viewpoints involved. As the director, one looks *with* the searching,
analytical eye of the lens which is set to obey his commands; as an actor, one is at the mercy of the camera. If
I am asked to appear in a still photograph or a movie
scene, I ask, "Where shall I stand, which way shall I look?"
If I may indulge in a bit of simplification, I believe that,
more than any other factor, this difference explains the
apparent disparity in emotional makeup of those pur-
suing the two crafts.

I have never completely understood how a performer
playing the leading role in a film can also successfully take
on the job of director. I know it has been done, sometimes
with singular results (e.g., Charles Chaplin, Orson Welles,
Laurence Olivier), but the sparseness of outstanding examples in itself helps support my claim. This is not to say
that a star performer should not turn his hand to directing if he feels so inclined. I am only puzzled when he
assumes both roles in the same production.

I am reminded of an incident that best illustrates this
point. A friend of mine who has played many leading
roles in his time has also a long list of directing jobs
among his credits. When he is not busy at either of these,
he fills his days writing screenplays. It was on such a chore
that I called on him to help lick a particularly unruly
script. We were within one week of finishing the script
when he was offered a good part in a film for about double

the salary he was getting as a writer. The part he was to play did not start for ten days. I thought this rather fortunate as it would give him time to finish his work on the script but he informed me that he would have to quit the writing job at once. He explained that he could not finish as a scriptwriter on Saturday and start out as an actor on Monday. I wanted to know why not. He said it would take a whole week to readjust his thinking. He said that in the writing job he had concerned himself with all the problems of the entire production: writing, casting, directing, locations, budget, schedules, etc.; while as an actor he wanted to think of none of them. When I asked what exactly he had in mind, he said, "I will go stay at a friend's house in Malibu next week. Twice a day, I will go in for a swim in the ocean, twice a day I will walk along the beach passing all the other homes and I will expand my chest and get it beautifully tanned."

When I tried to get him to settle for three days, he said, "I know, I've been there before. It takes me exactly one week to learn how to be a son-of-a-bitch."

I have just seen a delightful film, *Kotch,* directed by Jack Lemmon. And why not? He brought to the making of the film a world of valuable experience which is so often lacking in much film making today. I am grateful to Mr. Lemmon that he didn't also want to play the leading role.

In my opinion, Charles Chaplin is one of the greatest actors that ever lived. I have seen him do spontaneous mimicry that was incredible in its depth and perception. And yet, I have always thought that his direction fell far short of the high quality he always showed as an actor. The essential point is that the actor-director has to move in two different directions, a difficult thing at best.

One friend who was a big star in silent films and in

the early days of talkies explains the problem of appearing before the camera like this: "The movie camera is an infallible lie detector. You just don't dare try to deceive it. It catches your inner thoughts with more alertness than the most penetrating psychoanalyst." I have always believed that this was due to the tremendous enlargement the human figure must endure when film is projected onto a screen. And yet, the television medium with its comparatively smaller screen seems to expose a lot of hypocrisy in aspiring politicians who refuse to appear on TV for fear of being found out. In both cases it is probably due to the focused isolation of the close-up. The medium must be the message.

As I see it, the actor's problem is that he must temporarily set aside his own personality and limitations to assume the individuality supplied by the scriptwriter. If the assumed character expands the personality of the actor, playing the role can give him an exhilarating lift which he must partially abandon at the end of the day. This daily shuttling between one's self and someone else can be traumatic in itself. Unless an actor is well oriented psychologically the daily return to himself can be, to say the least, disheartening. A psychiatrist friend once facetiously defined a neurosis as "something that was dissoluble in two ounces of alcohol." When movies went through the total transformation from silent to sound and John Gilbert was given no more parts to play, he suddenly found that he had to live alone with himself. His life had not prepared him for this shock and his physician tried to relieve his turmoil with sedatives. He was isolated from film making while still a splendid romantic actor and died while still a rather young man.

Needless to say, the foregoing problem of identity is not the sole property of the acting profession. Movie directors as well as doctors, lawyers, architects, politicians

—indeed, all humans who play big parts—are required to to make the same daily transition to reality. Perhaps that fact accounts for the invention of the cocktail hour.

When he was asked if he believed that a man could be a very good actor if he's happy and satisfied, Jean-Louis Trintignant, who came to full recognition in the film *Z* and is one of France's leading film stars, gave this interesting answer:

> No, I don't think so. First of all, if a man is happy and satisfied he doesn't *want* to be an actor. Happy people can find so many more interesting, calmer things to do. I don't believe there's an actor whose 'sensitivity' isn't made up out of complexes. Certainly there are lots of people who have complexes and who aren't actors. But that's only because they haven't had the opportunity to become one. Acting is a minor form of art; it may be the *most* insignificant form. But it is, nevertheless, an art if it's done with a certain amount of dignity. Actors are only interpreters, secondhand creators. They create, but only for something that already exists. Of course, their work can have an artistic value. Basically, I became an actor because I was not gifted in any other art. If I could have played a musical instrument just a little bit, or if I could have drawn or sculpted, I would definitely have preferred to be a real creator.
> [From an interview with Phillippe Grumback, *Saturday Review*, February 26, 1972.]

On the subject of actors and acting I believe the closest to the truth would be to say that there is no categorizing or generalizing about them. I'll give you a few examples from my experience and you can form an opinion of your own.

LILLIAN GISH

Lillian Gish was the type of star who worked very closely with the chief cinematographer. In fact, it was she who brought H. Sartov into the studio as part of her contract. In the D. W. Griffith school, she learned the tremendous value of the exquisitely photographed close-up and she would sit patiently under the lights for a full hour or so while Sartov jockeyed the lamps to a hundred positions. Most lighting is done with stand-ins and stars are called upon to sit in the lights only for a brief checking period just prior to the making of the scene. Not so with Lillian. If she felt that the cinematographer might do a better job of lighting her delicate features, she would dispense with the stand-in and assume the job herself. If Sartov asked Lillian to play an entire scene without changing the angle of her head, she would readily consent. (See photo 6.)

Miss Gish was an artist who spared herself in no way. She threw herself wholeheartedly into everything she did, even dying. She wanted to know well in advance when we would film her death scene in *La Bohème* (1925). She wanted to get in the mood and stay in it. This caused me some alarm. Perhaps as a precautionary measure, I decided I had better schedule it on the last day of shooting. She asked for three days' notice, and Jack Gilbert and I watched Lillian grow paler and paler, thinner and thinner. (See photo 17.)

When she arrived on the set that fateful day, we saw her sunken eyes, her hollow cheeks, and we noticed that her lips had curled outward and were parched with dryness. What on earth had she done to herself? I ventured to ask about her lips and she said in syllables hardly audible that she had succeeded in removing all saliva from her mouth by not drinking any liquids for three days, and by keeping cotton pads between her teeth and gums even in her sleep.

A pall began to settle over the entire company. People moved about the stage on tiptoe and spoke only in whispers. Finally the scene came in which Rudolph carries the exhausted Mimi to her little bed and her Bohemian friends gather around while Mimi breathes her last. I let the camera continue on her lifeless form and the tragic faces around her and decided to call "cut" only when Miss Gish would be forced to inhale after holding her breath to simulate death. But the familiar movement of the chest didn't come. She neither inhaled nor exhaled. I began to fear she had played her part too well, and I could see that the other members of the cast and crew had the same fears as I. Too stunned to speak the one word that would halt the movement of the camera, I wondered how to bridge this fantastic moment back to the coldness of reality. The thought flashed through my mind, "What will the headlines say?" After what seemed many, many minutes, I waved my hand before the camera as a signal to stop. Still there was no movement from Lillian.

John Gilbert bent close, and softly whispered her name. Her eyes slowly opened. She permitted herself her first deep breath since the scene had started: for the past days she had trained herself, somehow or other, to get along without visible breathing. She had to wet her lips before she could speak. By this time there was no one on the set whose eyes were dry.

JENNIFER JONES

When I first saw Jennifer, I was impressed by the fact that her emotional reactions registered so clearly on her face. It is difficult to exactly define this quality. Perhaps plasticity does it. Does one classify her as a great actress or a great instrument? It was necessary to start her in the right mood each day by telling her the story of her part up to that moment; and it was advisable to keep her that way by talking to her from time to time throughout the day. Whatever gentleness and patience the director expended on Jennifer, he was rewarded a hundred-fold with a sensitive and intriguing performance. Whenever she played a scene with a feeling of insecurity, it showed in some strange tricks that she did with her mouth. It was the director's responsibility to make certain that this didn't happen. There was no excuse for a director who couldn't keep her in the proper mood and get a wonderful performance from her. (Jennifer Jones appeared in two of my films—*Duel in the Sun* and *Ruby Gentry*.)

CLARK GABLE

The perfect symbol of the all-male male but with more of a twinkle in the eye than most of the he-man types, John Wayne, for example. It was perhaps a sense of humor along with his sex appeal that explained his popularity. A complete pro in his function on the set and in communicating with the director—meaning that he was always on time, knew his lines, cooperated and willingly did what the script called for. (He worked with me in *Comrade X*.)

HEDY LAMARR

Her beauty made up for whatever she lacked in acting ability. Like Jennifer Jones, the director had to use patience in getting a performance out of Hedy. Acting probably didn't come naturally to her but the note of unsureness in what she did seemed to give her a certain childish attractiveness. Her interest seemed to be divided between the part she was playing and another career as an inventor or discoverer of some fascinating new soft drink or useful invention. Although Hedy was a tremendous sex symbol to millions of movie-goers, she presented quite a different image to those working with her on the set.

This is illustrated by an incident that occurred after a finish-of-the-picture party of a film in which Hedy was the star. When I arrived home about two hours late for dinner, my wife was in a forgiving mood but she couldn't help calling attention to some lip rouge on my shirt collar. My defensive reply which came forth quite spontaneously was, "Don't worry, it was only Hedy."

BARBARA STANWYCK

A professional's professional, a superb technician with a voice quality that immediately hooked you with its humanness. She was a big favorite with all her co-workers on the set as well as the public, and rightly so. From a director's viewpoint, a joy to work with—no problems.

AUDREY HEPBURN

Audrey played Natasha in *War and Peace* for me. During the years since that film was made and several years before, no one has ever crossed my mind who could have so admirably suited the part. While making the film, it often occurred to me that Audrey, though ideal from my viewpoint, would probably not fulfill a Russian's concept of the part. And yet when the film was made in Russia a few years later, they cast an actress that was exactly Audrey's type. Audrey studied ballet as a child and moves through a scene with a rhythmic grace that is a director's delight. Whenever I am asked that most embarrassing of all questions—"Who is your favorite actress of all those you have directed?"—one always comes immediately to mind.

ROBERT DONAT

Now that I've talked about one of my favorite actresses I'm going to follow it up with one of my top favorites among the men.

I had been hearing much about the clauses in the contract demanded by the romantic star Robert Donat before he would consider doing the role of Dr. Manson in *The Citadel*. By the time I reached London, his conditions had all been accepted. I was anxious to meet Mr. Donat, and a luncheon was arranged at the Carlton Hotel.

I sat there anticipating an entrance in the bouncing Douglas Fairbanks or swashbuckling Errol Flynn manner. Instead I saw a frail, hollow-chested fellow in a Norfolk jacket and tweed cap standing in the doorway. He carried a battered briefcase and looked more like a shy book-keeper or reticent bank clerk than the romantic star I had seen on the screen. He spoke in soft, almost whispered, tones as if protecting his voice. His intake breathing was audible due to an asthmatic condition. In the briefcase he carried notes and comments on the book and the script, sketches for the clothes he would wear, and photographic suggestions for some of the Welsh locations we would need. He wanted to go with me to Wales when I visited the mines and mining towns. (See photo 21.) This is a most unusual attitude for a member of a cast, but Bob Donat was the most helpful and cooperative star with whom I have ever worked, as well as one of the finest actors. He is the only actor I have ever known who had a graph of his character development charted out on the wall of his dressing room. This chart also meticulously indicated each small change in his dress.

As work on the new picture became all-absorbing, his figure straightened, his chest filled, his voice became clear, color appeared in his cheeks. The making of a film often has its therapeutic value, and over a period of years I have observed that the psychological reasons for hard work are often more dynamic than artistic ones, though of course the two are tied closely together.

The most startling thing to me was his attention to what seemed infinitesimal and unimportant details of his appearance. A stray hair behind one of his ears, a touch of red make-up under the tip of his nose, a line on his forehead would seem to absorb all of his attention up to the moment the actual shooting of the scene began. Then, instantaneously, he would start to act and the perfection of his performance would astound me. The minute I said "Cut," he would pick up a mirror from some concealed place on the set and return to the business of examining the hair behind his ears.

TYRONE POWER

I seem to be grouping all the good guys together but there are more to come. Ty was really a handsome man without being pretty, a fine actor to boot and one of the most considerate in his relations with me.

In 1959, as we were filming *Solomon and Sheba* I felt he was giving his best performance; I also thought that the completed picture would have been his best. He died when it was only half-finished. It is a shame that even the completed footage couldn't be released for television.

HENRY FONDA

A convincing performer in a rather confined and restrained manner. His middle western inflection and accent makes you think that he is a down-to-earth man but often he comes across quite differently. During the

filming of *War and Peace* after I had taken a long time
explaining some of the motivations Tolstoy had given the
character of Pierre, Fonda said to me, "I have been
listening to you for almost an hour and I still don't know
what the hell you are talking about and doubt if I ever
will."

On occasion, I arranged to accompany him on the hour's
ride to and from the location site in order to get to know
him better, but I never did. Something going on here that
takes a better psychoanalyst than I am to fathom. However, some sort of hang-up usually makes for a more interesting performance on the screen.

ROBERT YOUNG

Here is a superb actor without a single problem, at
least none that I was ever able to detect. Bob is completely
on top of his profession. On the set he behaves with confi-
dence, security and total control. In his early career, I
used to think that he moved with such ease that no woman would ever want to mother him. This conviction his
screen image projects has paid off well in the character he
plays in his television series. (He worked with me in *H. M.
Pulham, Esq.* and *Northwest Passage*.)

GARY COOPER

An easy-going, silent, slow-moving type but comes on
strong when the chips are down. Every woman wanted to
mother and care for him. When I say *every*, I mean *every*
woman. Gary was really photogenic, long shot, medium or
close-up. I remember the first small part he played on the
screen in a silent film called *The Winning of Barbara
Worth*. You didn't have to be a genius to see immediately
that here was someone who had what it takes. I also remember well the first day I directed him in one of my

films called *Wedding Night*. He had difficulty remember-
ing or speaking two or three sentences consecutively. We
had to stop the camera again and again and put the scene
together piecemeal. This was one of his early speaking
parts: he had not needed words before to communicate.
When I saw the rushes next day, all the problems faded
away. I was astonished at what came through on the
screen.

By the time of *The Fountainhead*, he was handling difficult dialogue expertly. He may have played Gary Cooper
in every role but his image was so valuable that it was
worth rewriting any role to suit him. There simply could
not have been a more pleasant fellow to work with than
Gary Cooper. (He worked with me in *Wedding Night* and
The Fountainhead.)

KIRK DOUGLAS

Kirk comes across with aggressive strength. It is rather
difficult, I imagine, to project an aggressive image in scene
after scene all day from nine to six and not have some of
it rub off on yourself. I felt throughout the filming of *Man
Without a Star* that Kirk was working himself up to being
a director and couldn't help, in studying a scene the night
before, figuring out the way he would do it if he were
directing. This sometimes causes minor conflicts since the
director has probably planned the scene weeks before and
is usually not in the mood to make last minute changes.
Along with the aggressiveness, Kirk is a tireless worker
and a first-rate performer.

YUL BRYNNER

Very much in the Kirk Douglas category although with
the suggestion of an Oriental approach. Brynner made his
first big hit in *The King and I* for which he was ideally

cast. However, he seems to have been influenced by this part ever since. Still, I never saw him before that time and maybe the role of the King of Siam was bent to fit an already established Brynner. Brynner likes to play strong, aristocratic, unwavering characters who are not troubled with indecision—in short—kings. Cecil B. De Mille seemed to be his favorite director. Many of the leading characters in my films must wrestle with the two sides of their psyche. In *Solomon and Sheba,* the core of the story was Solomon's inner struggle to choose between his responsibilities as head of state and church and his yearning to satisfy his sensual desires with the pagan queen. Tyrone Power had understood the dualistic problem of the anguished king. When Brynner took over after his death he fought the idea of a troubled monarch and wanted to dominate each situation without conflict. It was an attitude that affected the depth of his performance and probably the integrity of the film. I have no quarrel with an actor upholding the image he most successfully projects but when he is offered a part that is fundamentally in conflict with that image, then his first consideration should be to the quality of the picture.

LAURETTE TAYLOR

She had a unique style of acting that has never been duplicated. A superb comedienne with a bounce and piquant way of doing things. The characters she played were not confined to her actual age at the time; she was equally convincing in roles half or double her age. Her laughing, bubbling style brought her thousands of admirers for her performances on both the stage and in films.

JOHN GILBERT

Gilbert, known as the great lover in his day, always gave an energetic and intense performance. Acting was his life and in his private life he always lived the role he was playing on the screen: when he was playing a Russian character, he ate Russian food, wore Russian clothes and had a balalaika orchestra performing on the terrace outside of his bedroom window while he made love to some young and beautiful hopeful. It is generally believed, or so the story goes, that when sound came in his voice was too high and after two or three pictures he was kept off the screen even though he was under contract for a very large salary at Metro-Goldwyn-Mayer.

I strongly disagree with this theory of the high voice and I explain his downfall in another way. His type of love-making was so intense and aggressive that when it came to putting words to his actions the result turned out to be funny instead of serious. John Gilbert was a casualty of talking films. Imagine in a hot love scene speaking the words "I adore you, I worship you, I love you"—not good enough—better to let each individual member of the audience supply the words to his own taste. Had he known enough in the beginning to play the scenes without dialogue, perhaps John Gilbert's popularity would have survived.

A thoroughly likeable and pleasant man though a victim of his own neuroses. When he was paid large sums of money for doing nothing, it was a slap in the face to him. He came to me with a desire to work as a second assistant. The despair of inactivity caused him gradually to become dependent upon sedatives and this probably contributed greatly to his early death. Gilbert was an example of an actor giving his all for the parts he played. Because

of this he had lost all contact with the strength of his own
individuality; and when he had no part telling him what
to do, in his loneliness he lost all sense of direction. (He
worked with me in *The Big Parade, La Bohème, Wife of
the Centaur, Bardelys, the Magnificent.*)

RONALD COLMAN

The first of the expatriate Britishers to use an impec-
cable manner of speaking in American films. Colman
possessed a distinctly individual style. In life he was the
same sophisticated gentleman he played on the screen. A
superb actor and yet confined within the limits of his aristocratic image.

SPENCER TRACY

Tracy along with Robert Donat just about head my list
of the best actors I've worked with. Everything that Spence
did came over with tremendous conviction. This was his
biggest asset. Like Gilbert, he had to deal constantly with
emotional problems. One time he traveled to Europe by
ship keeping the doctor up all night, every night just for
company and conversation. When the ship reached Naples
he did not want to get off and stayed on until it returned
to New York City. He played strong courageous parts with
absolute conviction and yet physically—and emotionally—
he was hardly a strong, courageous man. While working in
Idaho on a tough location for *Northwest Passage,* he repeatedly threatened to leave the location and return to
Los Angeles before the job was finished. I had to use several unusual methods to placate his fears and calm him
into finishing the location work. (See photo 31.) I am sad
to have to say that what gives many actors' work interest

and vitality is the conflict between their own tumultuous emotional lives and the outer role they are playing.

GREGORY PECK

A fine actor and citizen. Greg is blessed with a superb speaking voice. I have at times heard him criticized in some roles for exhibiting a stiffness, a lack of ease. And yet when I directed him in *Duel in the Sun* I found him as flexible and pliable as any actor with whom I have worked. I modeled the character of Lewt in *Duel* somewhat after Sportin' Life in *Porgy and Bess*. Greg was delighted with the idea and gave an intriguing performance that made a vivid impression with the public. Gregory Peck has been president of the Academy of Motion Picture Arts and Sciences and takes a large interest in public affairs. Who knows, he may one day be governor of California!

BETTE DAVIS

One of the screen's top actresses who probably couldn't help conjuring up a reputation of being difficult to handle. I got along with her fine in the film called *Beyond the Forest* until one morning I corrected the manner in which she was hurling a small bottle of medicine. I tried to show her the way I felt it should be done which would give more strength to her action. She resented my directions and unbeknownst to me went to the head of the studio and told them that unless I was taken off the picture she would not appear for work the next day. When the executives told her that they were pleased with my work and that I would not be taken off the film, she countered with the fact that she would come to work the next day only if they would cancel her contract. At this time, she had been with the studio eighteen years, had been a very successful star for the Warner Bros. studio but her box office potential was dwindling rapidly. They gladly jumped at the chance to cancel the remaining years of her contract and she returned to work the next day. I was told of these shenanigans only on the last day of shooting for fear that the revelation might impair our relationship and thus the quality of the film. At the farewell dinner on the last evening of shooting, she told me that she had loved working with me and would be happy to work in any other stories I found that suited her. Such are the problems of film making and of working with Miss Bette Davis.

GINA LOLLOBRIGIDA

I believe she was born in Naples and started her career as a dressmaker and designer of women's clothes. I think this was one of her greatest obstacles because she had a hard time accepting the clothes designed by anyone else. In my book, she, along with Hedy Lamarr, is one of the most beautiful women in films. When she was working with Tyrone Power who behaved on the set with such decorum, she matched his mood and was a joy to direct but when Yul Brynner came on the film after Ty's death and started to throw his weight around, Gina changed her behavior, apparently feeling that she had to keep up with Brynner. It always seemed to me that her own life was one of struggle like the life of so many Neopolitans who have to fight for every lira and crust of bread. This struggle has carried over into her adult life and she believes that she has to fight for each close-up, each extra scene, and each concession from the cameraman and the director. On the other hand she is one of the few actresses to understand her image better than anyone else and is able to do a superior job with her makeup and hair dressing. The same might be true of her costumes if it were not so upsetting to the schedule.

Editor's Note: (In addition to the foregoing, Mr. Vidor has directed the following stars and leading players):

Colleen Moore	Lionel Barrymore
Florence Vidor	Margaret Sullivan
Zasu Pitts	Rosalind Russell
Eleanor Boardman	Ralph Richardson
Renée Adorée	Rex Harrison
James Murray	Brian Donlevy
Marion Davies	Joseph Cotton
Wallace Beery	Walter Huston
Marie Dressler	Charlton Heston
Jackie Cooper	Walter Brennan
Sylvia Sidney	Karl Malden
Beulah Bondi	

After working in synchronous sound films for a number of years with its usual dependence on dialogue, the techniques of directing actors in silent films began to fade in my memory. I wondered exactly what I had told them to do and just how they accomplished what they did. I knew some stars had earned tremendous salaries, many equal to current ones (relatively speaking), with the production costs today being eight or ten times what they were then. But just what did they do to warrant those large salaries? I remembered that the directors often guided them with brief instructions while the shooting of the scene was actually taking place. Some directors talked during the scene more than others. Commands had to be sharp and clear so that they would penetrate an actor's consciousness without causing confusion. But to what extent was the director responsible for the performance of the actors as compared with today's talk-oriented performances?

Recently, in running my old films in connection with an Oral History Program of The American Film Institute, I have had some revealing thoughts about this dilemma. It seems that the art of pantomime with its emphasis on gesture, facial expression and body language served to bring out the unique individuality of each performer in a sharper degree than today's at least partial dependence on words.

I believe that an outstanding performance was much more difficult to achieve in the "silents" than in the "talkies"; I believe that getting an acceptable performance out of an inexperienced novice presented far greater difficulties than that of getting an acceptable reading of a pre-studied dialogue scene. The art of silent-picture acting could not be learned overnight—and there were no cue cards to tell you what to do. Very many persons can read dialogue properly in one or two run-throughs. The proper reading of a line will give you almost all the accompanying facial and body expressions you need, but try this with pantomime.

If you want to make your personal test of what I am saying, organize a game of Pantomime Quiz some evening and watch the nervous jitters take hold of your more timid friends. When they are having their most difficult time in expressing themselves pantomimically, they will try to fall back on a few grunts or whatever other sounds they may get away with to help them out.

Charlie Chaplin, perhaps the greatest of all pantomimists the world has ever known, was simply dreadful in playing "The Game," as Pantomime Quiz was called when it was the rage in Hollywood. And yet, as I have already said, he could jump spontaneously into a superb pantomimic characterization of any prominent person or any one of his friends without a moment's preparatory thought. I have no explanation for this paradox except that in one case he was entirely on his own as a performer and in the other he was part of a group under compulsion to act out the words of a second group on the opposing side.

Loretta Young was the most enthusiastic and probably the best at playing "The Game." I participated and watched with tremendous interest. Here were people who had formerly made a career out of voiceless acting but who could be either wonderful or terrible in another form of the same craft. Is it because on the screen they had learned to play themselves and in another form they were helpless?

This learned ability to perform one's inner psyche without the use of words had a kind of magic about it. A star was known by the self that he symbolized to his public and bad luck to the star who changed his image midstream. The loyal supporters felt betrayed. Every star at some time in his career wants to play a different role from the one with which he has become identified. He wants to prove the versatility of his acting ability. If he is in a position of sufficient power, he usually gets his way. In most cases the result is tragic or, at best, frustrating.

This playing of one's self has very little to do with what is known as acting but it accounted for more major box-office stars than are developed in the films of today. It took large studios and strong-minded executives to hold ambitious stars to a series of self-identification films. When the plans and power of the large studios began to disintegrate, the star system followed the same path. Each single film had to stand or fall on its own merits. Long range image exploitation came to a standstill. The number of top stars today can be counted on the fingers of one hand.

CHAPTER 4

THROUGH
THE CAMERA'S EYE

◉

During the golden years of Hollywood, feminine stars usually put a tremendous emphasis on their chief cinematographer. When a cameraman had learned all the tricks of lighting a star's face she would insist that he come along with her as part of a package which usually included her hairdresser, her make-up man and costume designer. Garbo had William Daniels, Colleen Moore was photographed by George Folsey, Mae Murray had Oliver Marsh. By carefully watching the electricians the stars learned what arrangement of lights suited them best.

I first became acquainted with the importance of this when I understook the job of directing Laurette Taylor in *Peg O' My Heart*. Miss Taylor had been starring in the stage play for quite a few years when the Metro Company made a deal for her and the play. I was a young director who needed some income in order to get my very small studio out of the greedy hands of a most unethical lawyer. It was not a question of who should play the part—it was Laurette Taylor or no one. Her husband was the author of the play and together they owned all rights.

The character Laurette Taylor performed in the play was an Irish girl of eighteen or nineteen years. At the time she was forty-two and had a reputation as somewhat of an imbiber. The legitimate stage had been kind to her but what would happen when her face and figure had to withstand the critical examination and tremendous enlargement of the motion picture screen?

I had never seen her on the stage nor met her in person. I was most anxious to see what she looked like. The first film test that arrived from New York was photographed by Billy Bitzer, D. W. Griffith's famous cameraman. Nevertheless, instead of looking eighteen or even forty-two, she looked sixty. She had chosen to wear a curly wig in the test and this in itself could have been responsible for adding ten or fifteen years. Her frightened face hung down like an old lace curtain. I suppose that first test added fifteen or twenty years to my twenty-two, at least for the rest of the day. But there we were and although I began to see it as an impossible task, I knew that there was no backing out of it, or recasting the part, or abandoning the film.

In desperation I remembered a day's retake because of bad photography on my previous film. On this occasion I had jokingly said, when I noticed the photographer of the still photos standing idle all day, "If it is a question of bad lighting, why is it we don't have to retake all the still photos?" In looking at the still pictures I found that the feminine lead in the film looked as beautiful as ever on that particular day when retakes were ordered. What was the reason? The lens of the still camera had a peculiar distortion which gave a roundness to the face instead of the harsh reality of the newsreel type of lens used on the movie camera.

I put the next question to George Barnes, the photographer whom we had chosen for the unhappy job of photographing the Taylor film. Barnes was still trying to catch his breath after viewing the Bitzer test. I said, "George, is it possible to photograph 35mm movies through the lens of an 8-by-10 still camera?" He replied, "I've never heard of it but we can certainly try."

We found the still cameraman working with his flattering distorting lens at another studio on another film. We had to do our experimenting at night so that he and his camera could be back at work in the morning. As I remember, the final and most successful test was made with the movie camera by photographing through the 8-by-10 ground glass of the still camera. We were ready with our trick lens to perform a miracle.

The day after our forty-two-year-old star arrived in California with maid, poodle dog, and playwright husband we started a series of photographic tests to see if what we were trying to do was somewhere within the realm of possibility. Barnes, with the help of his chief electrician, rigged up a spotlight with rifle sights. This spot was mounted on a six-foot platform (or parallel) and an electrician assigned to keep Miss Taylor's face in the small circle of light at all times. The brightness of the light served to wash out all shadows and wrinkles on the star's face regardless of her position. Because of its height above the stage floor, it threw a false shadow around our subject's aging chin. This manufactured chin line working with the distorted funhouse-mirror lens began to subtract the years like an expert face-lift. And speaking of face lifts, the following trick was my final trump card. When Laurette was amused and laughing the inside muscles of her neck and jaws tightened up becomingly. If I could only keep her this way for the duration of a scene, we would have it made. I came to work each day with a good supply of jokes and gags. I instructed the crew to keep the set light and gay and the musicians to play only happy and fast tempo tunes.

In the final film Laurette Taylor looked eighteen. In some of the scenes when all tricks worked together she could have passed for sixteen. She fell so much in love with the person she saw on the screen that she ran the picture night after night for her friends in her New York home on Riverside Drive. One time after many such screenings she

invited Ethel Barrymore to come to dinner. Miss Barrymore's secretary called back with this message, "Miss
Barrymore accepts with pleasure if she is assured that she
will not have to sit through *Peg O' My Heart* again."

I am considering the truth of Flip Wilson's favorite line
"What you see is what you get," as it applies to a movie
camera. What you see with your eyes is three dimensional
but what you get through a camera lens is two dimensional. But this seeming restriction is only half the story.
To compensate for this seeming limitation the film maker
will try to extend his product to *four* dimensions. Giving
the recorded image the feeling of being in three dimensions is not terribly difficult. This can be accomplished
through lighting, a moving shot, the proper use of color,
focal definition, moving people and objects, and natural
and unnatural uses of the laws of perspective. You are
going to ask me "What are the unnatural uses of perspective?" Well, for one, *forced perspective*.

In my film *The Crowd* I showed a scene of an ex-
pectant father in a hospital corridor. We wanted the
hallway to look much longer than it was practical to construct on a studio stage, so we made each successive doorway shorter. At the far end of the set, door frames were
only about 4½ or 5 feet high. To keep these small doors
from being betrayed by full size people we employed little
people, even a few dwarfs, to work in the back of the set.

Forced perspective was also used in *The Crowd* to
achieve a tunnel-like effect. A young boy, at the death of
his father, felt the approaching burden of new responsi-
bilities and this was symbolized by having him slowly
climb a very long stairway. The stairway we built was
actually a long one but the walls apparently surrounding
it were only painted in forced perspective on a flat surface
at the bottom of the stairs.

Each lens of a varying focal length creates a different feeling of depth and perspective. How many times have you seen a photograph of an automobile in which it appears twice as long as it actually is? A wide-angle lens, for example 25mm, will almost double the depth of the objects in a scene. Therefore, if someone moves from the background to the foreground, he will appear to be moving twice as fast as he actually is, i.e., covering the lengthened distance in the same amount of time. Though purely illusory, you see what you get rather than getting what you see. (See photos 18 and 27.)

The longer focal length lenses have precisely the opposite effect. The background is brought nearer to the foreground. One might surmise that because of this quality the depth of focus would be greater. The reverse is true. In most scenes taken with a long focal lens the near and far background are completely out of focus. These lenses are often chosen to achieve this kind of portrait effect. The 50mm lens is considered to be the one that most nearly approximates the vision of the human eye. The extreme wide-angle lens is often called a "bug-eye" lens. I suppose this explains why it is so difficult to get close to a cockroach or a housefly.

Now about the fourth dimension. In the scene from *The Crowd* already mentioned, the one in which the young boy climbed the long stairway, another dimension was added, an emotional nuance that is not referred to in the script. I could, no doubt, cite hundreds of instances in which directors or cinematographers have added another dimension to their scenes. Chaplin often made you feel sorrow in the midst of a comedy routine and many directors literally infuse their films with thought-provoking content that is above and beyond the scene itself.

In Antonioni's *Blow-Up* or Resnais' *Last Year at Mar-*

ienbad or Fellini's *8½* there was much more than what merely met the eye. We return to consider the individuality of the film maker: how he lives, what he dreams about, how much of his unconscious is revealed in front of the camera.

A director is not always conscious that these inner or hidden motives are weaving themselves into his scenes. I have on occasion been interviewed about one of my films long after it was made and the interviewer has brought up meanings and interpretations which I doubt that I had ever been thoroughly aware of before. Yet they were unmistakably of my doing. There is so much of one's own living that goes into his work that it behooves every craftsman-artist to open his doors to all reality.

In the beginning, the camera was thought of as an immovable object to be placed on some sort of stand or tripod and left there. This concept was an outgrowth of the old portrait studio with its high-backed chair or family settee. The first movie sets were just as static; even the first studios were constructed in the shape of one camera angle, the medium-long shot. It wasn't until Griffith started moving in for close-ups that directors realized that movie cameras could move. It was thought previous to this time that if the camera cut the actors off at the waist, knees, or ankles, the scene would look more like an operating room in a hospital than a platform for drama.

The technique of camera set-ups, even in later Hollywood days, followed a pattern of long shot, medium shot, close-ups. This practice was so routine in the silent picture era that writers believed they could designate all camera set-ups in their scripts. I never could determine an exact camera shot until I coordinated it with the movement on the set, and I could never understand how a writer sitting before a typewriter could determine it.

The reason for the long shot was to show the entire set wall-to-wall. The studio had built the set for this production and the bosses wanted the directors to show where they had spent their money—as if anyone in the audience would give a damn.

Then came a medium shot of the actors in the scene. The camera would record the entire scene from this angle —little or no panning being permitted and certainly no perambulating or zooming. These two techniques were still awaiting the enlightenment brought by the evolution of film making to come.

Then came a series of straight-on close-ups of each participant in the scene. The purpose of these were two-fold: first, to be used as accents in the medium shots; second, to give complete freedom to the editor in the cutting room. This freedom included the ability to rearrange or eliminate parts of the scene at the request of the producer —generally after a preview or two.

John Ford was one of the first directors I heard of who was "cutting with the camera" on the set. This meant that he photographed only that part of the scene that he wanted to see in the final picture. I had been more or less easing into this technique when I heard about Ford's methods. I had eliminated the long shot made for the sake of showing the set, and had skipped many of the covering close-ups. I was evolving a form I regarded as "flowing composition," which meant that I would shoot several pages of script dialogue without stopping the camera, and yet be close enough to the actors so that insertion of individual close-ups was not necessary. I would not make covering close-ups so that the scene could not be altered in the cutting room by an over-ambitious editor or producer. "Flowing composition" had to be done with a camera on a dolly. Its up and down movement was regulated by a small boom. Both these innovations have now come into widespread use. In fact, when the first German films arrived containing much mobile camera-work, a big cry went up from some directors and many producers that they were getting dizzy from too much motion. Some top executives sent out studio directives that they wanted the cameras stationary. Had directors obeyed the order, we would have slipped back to the beginning.

Today the trend is to more and more hand-held camera technique. At a recent festival, I saw an interesting Cuban film in which the use of a hand-held camera added greatly to the interest of the picture and helped win it the top award. In a hand-to-hand fight between soldiers on horseback, the camera was right in the thick of it, moving in all directions and up and down as the action dictated. It seems that the photographer must have been mounted on horseback as well.

In another scene in the same film, a crazed prostitute starts a scene in an erect position, but eventually is clawing at the gravel of the street. The camera executes a beautiful descending movement keeping her head in a close-up throughout the action. It could have been done with a small boom, but I think the camera was hand-held in this case too.

CHAPTER 5

SCHEDULES AND BUDGETS

■•■

One of the most necessary—and helpful—phases of movie production is the schedule and budget. An accurate budget cannot be made until a working schedule has been carefully prepared. Until the screenplay goes onto the schedule board, all the scenes and sequences are considered in chronological order. When the production manager breaks the script down, it must be considered from an economic and practical viewpoint. One can readily see how unwise it would be to shoot a scene in a set on the second day of production; then, supposing no scenes occur there until near the end of the film, that particular set would be left idle for six to eight weeks. The procedure would tie up the lighting equipment, the furnishings, the valuable stage space, besides the cost of the time lost in moving the company and all the mobile equipment out of the set and back again at some later date. There is still another consideration that could make this kind of operation more costly than those listed above. Let us presume that one of the important members of the cast works only in this particular interior setting. Say that he works only five days in the entire film, three days in the early part of the film and two days near the end. If the director insisted upon shooting in direct story continuity, the actor would work three days, then sit on his fanny for six to eight weeks, on full salary, until he went to work again for two days later on. A fine bonanza for the actor at two thousand dollars per week, but hell on the film's budget. The Screen Actor's Guild contract does not permit their members to go on and off salary to complete a part in one film.

Therefore, the production manager's number one consideration in arranging his schedule is to keep the interior sets and individual members of the cast active once they start to function in the film.

A schedule board containing movable plastic strips each representing one day of production greatly facilitates the production manager's job. (See photos 24 and 25.)

Until the board is arranged in its final form, the day and date is left blank at the top of each strip which can be freely changed around to achieve the most efficient scheduling. Directly below this space is marked the name of the interior set or exterior location with scene numbers to be covered on a given shooting day.

On a wider space on the left of the board, each member of the cast is listed. Making an X-mark opposite each cast member's name on the narrow day strip indicates whether the actor works on that day or appears on the indicated location or set. A wide stretch of idle time on an actor's part will be readily observed on the board. The strips can then be rearranged so that the performer will start on salary as late as possible, will be utilized as steadily as practical, and his part completed without unnecessary delay.

In preparing *Duel in the Sun*, we thought Walter Huston would be ideal for the part of the itinerant preacher called the "Sinkiller." According to the schedule, this part could be completed in four days. There was only one Walter Huston and his agent was well aware of this fact. He demanded for the part a salary of $4,000 a week with a minimum of ten weeks. This meant that if we used him only four days he would be earning $10,000 for each day he worked. David Selznick, the producer of the film, who never thought much of economy where quality was concerned, decided to go ahead on Mr. Huston's terms. This meant that Mr. Huston was available to us for ten weeks without extra pay so we could use our conservation procedure for some other member of the cast.

Mr. Selznick became so intrigued with Mr. Huston's performance as the "Sinkiller" that he started writing him into other parts in the script. (By this time Selznick had also become the writer of the screenplay.) By adding scenes and by rewriting some of those already made, Mr. Huston's appearance eventually spanned a greater term than the original ten-week guarantee.

Perhaps more than any other item, the cost of producing a film is based on time. A schedule enables the cost estimator to figure the number of sets required, the number of location trips with possible housing and feeding on location, travel expense, length of time crew and cast will have to be on salary, and a hundred other items that go into the making of a film.

Of course there are a number of set charges that are not specifically accounted for on the basis of time. Some of these are cost of story, screenplay, stars, director. This part of a regular cost analysis sheet is referred to as "above-the-line" costs. These items are not so variable as those below-the-line.

All the minimum wage contracts with the talent guilds and the craft unions must be taken into consideration unless of course the film is to be an "underground" production which manages to circumvent these labor and guild requirements.

A recent movement in film production in the U.S.A. and in certain European countries is the participation deal. In this kind of production, all those contributing their talents and labor to the picture do so on a deferment of all or part of their salary with an equivalent percentage share in the net profits from the sale or distribution of the film. This plan greatly aids independent film making and because there is not such a large initial investment at stake offers greater freedom in the choice of story and cast. When a large studio risks two million dollars and upward on the cost of a film negative, they are going to demand certain safeguards and assurances. In the last few years, a number of potentially important films have been put together for a cash outlay of only $150,000 to $200,000. One can readily understand the release from tension that this difference in risk of capital would bring about.

Over the years, production costs, along with everything else, have become higher and higher. When I first arrived in Hollywood and got a job at Universal Studio as a company clerk, my salary was twelve dollars per week; later on I moved to the scenario writing deparment and my weekly salary jumped to forty dollars. At that time, total production costs at Universal were figured on a basis of one dollar per foot of film: a 5,000-foot feature could be made for $5,000. In 1925, I made a 12,000-foot film, *The Big Parade*, for $245,000. This film was largely responsible for establishing Metro-Goldwyn-Mayer as a major company. The last time I saw any figures, it had grossed over $22 million and was still going.

About the middle of the 1930s, Louis B. Mayer called all employees of M.G.M. together for a noontime meeting on one of the large stages. His plea was to ask for some relief from the steadily mounting costs. He said that their important features had risen to an unbelievable cost of $350,000. He declared emphatically that if they rose to $400,000 or $450,000 the company would be forced out of business. We didn't know it at the time but this meeting was a preliminary exercise to prepare us for a fifty percent salary cut by all studios in Hollywood. This little amalgamated caper had its direct and speedy result in the formation of all the talent guilds and unions.

Production costs continued their upward spiral but the studios, far from closing up shop, flourished even more than before.

Today the simplest film project gets budgeted at $1.5, $2, $3 million and from there on upward to $5, $10, $15, even $20 million. The same studio that feared bankruptcy if they spent over $350,000 has recently spent over $12 million on *Ryan's Daughter*.

In order to arrive at some comparative cost figures, it would be interesting to compare the early version of De Mille's *Ten Commandments* with the later one. The same could be done with M.G.M.'s *Mutiny on the Bounty* or with the first and second versions of *Stagecoach*. The fairly recent biblical film *The Greatest Story Ever Told* cost $22 million.

The steadily mounting costs of Hollywood film production have forced film packagers to seek any escape route to get a favorite story made into a motion picture. For a while Europe was a safe refuge, and in many respects still is. It would not be considered economical to transport a production requiring only a small cast and a few interior settings to Europe, but one requiring many extras and costumes and calling for much construction work can be made for a much smaller expenditure in Europe. Some examples, besides my own *War and Peace* and *Solomon and Sheba*, are *Quo Vadis, Ben Hur, Lawrence of Arabia, Dr. Zhivago, Nicholas and Alexandra,* and *Fiddler on the Roof*. In fact, the only very large American production that has been made in and around Los Angeles in recent years has been George Stevens' *The Greatest Story Ever Told*. Stevens made some sort of deal with the Screen Extra's Guild to avoid excessive overtime charges while working on Holy Land locations in Utah.

What is the reason for these constantly escalating costs in Hollywood? For many years the greatest amount of American film production was centered there. This meant the greatest concentration of artistic and technical talent. More demand for better qualified personnel meant a potential use of power when the various talent groups saw fit to amalgamate into guilds and unions. Top professionals in each group wielded their strength to carry the hopes and demands of the less talented. Adroit executives of large studios considered it the better part of good judgment to listen and to bargain. When a labor contract expires, new salaries and concessions are demanded. It seems that a guild or union would lose its status if an upward spiral of benefits did not result from each new contract.

Because of an unusual situation that exists in the centers of United States film production, it often happens that a producer-director or an actor-producer will find himself alternately wearing two hats and sitting on both sides of the bargaining table. On one side as a producer he is doing all he can to hold down mounting production costs, while on the other side he is fighting hard to drive the best bargain he can for the members of his guild. I doubt if this situation occurs in any other guild or union.

There is no question but that the actors', directors' and writers' guild enjoy the highest per capita income of any group of employees in the world. When I say that a guild member sits on both sides of the bargaining table I am not speaking literally. His sentiments are decidedly on the side of the guild, and he is willing to suffer the discomfort of rising costs in order to achieve the best possible conditions and compensations for his fellow workers.

The greatest impetus to the formation of the three top talent guilds were early attempts to use the Academy of Motion Picture Arts and Sciences as a channel to put through unilateral salary cuts. (The first instance of this has already been mentioned.) If an individual rose and protested he was, in the eyes of the top executives present, an immediate target for recrimination. A guild could speak as a unified organization without fear of censure to the individual.

Fortunately for the guilds, no power-hungry individual has ever come along and tried to take control. From my experience of talent guild operations I am convinced it would be impossible. The guilds are democratically governed by capable and intelligent men who are willing to spend days of their meager free time administering their organizations.

In speaking of power I am reminded of an evening at the home of Charlie Chaplin some years ago when he lived in Beverly Hills. Paulette Goddard, his wife at the time, had called to invite us to dinner saying that they were having an interesting guest and needed our help to entertain him. We arrived amidst the champagne and caviar to meet Harry Bridges, the spokesman for all West Coast longshoremen, who was accompanied by a young interference runner we will call Evans because I do not remember his name.

During the course of the evening the wine began to loosen the tongue of the cockney-accented Bridges and he started expounding his inner dreams. He told how before very long he would call a strike that would have all West Coast shippers groveling at his feet and this work stoppage would paralyze all western industry. Its crippling effect would be felt throughout the United States and eventually the whole world. He would ride down San Francisco's Market Street at the head of five thousand resolute and cheering men. It was one of the most succinct statements of power I have ever heard.

Paulette, who had the ability to go right to the point,

asked in a most gentle tone of inquiry, "But Mr. Bridges, how will the longshoremen feel about all this?"

Bridges was quick to reply, the wine probably drawing out his deepest sentiments, "Who gives a goddamn about how the men feel?"

It was time for Evans to step in. "What Mr. Bridges wants to point out is that the men don't always know what is best for them."

Paulette, apparently satisfied with the answer, poured more champagne.

The point that I want to make here is that I believe the members of the Hollywood guilds and unions are well able to decide what is best for them.

1. When sound first came to Hollywood, camera noise caused many problems. An early solution was to encase the cameras in thick padding (called "Bonnies" or "Barnies") in order to silence them.

2. Cumbersome technicolor and sound equipment made rhythmic, fluid camera movement difficult: it took eight men just to *move* the 800-pound camera used in this dolly shot from *Northwest Passage*.

3. This visually stunning silent love scene from *Bardelys the Magnificent* was improvised on location: the resourceful prop man was able to produce a period boat on request and a corridor of willow leaves was constructed in less than an hour.

4. Before process backgrounds were developed this complicated rig was necessary to shoot a scene inside a moving carriage.

5. Set-up for innovative sequence (1920) in which cameraman will shoot wild cattle stampeding overhead from beneath platform.

6. Vidor uses blue glasses to check lighting and color values on Lillian Gish's face. The naked eye could not predict the effect produced on the black and white film after processing.

8. *Right:* Karen Morley and Tom Keene (off camera) working on a love scene from *Our Daily Bread.* 9. *Below:* A still from the completed take. *Photo: M. S. Lacy.*

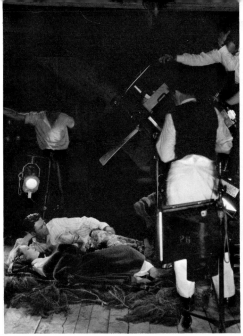

◀7. *Opposite:* Vidor, cameraman, assistant, and technicolor equipment on raised, mechanically operated platform. Vidor (with megaphone) is directing a scene from *Solomon and Sheba.*

10. *Left:* Vidor illustrates the relationship between the metronome beat, film footage, and a music score. 11. *Right:* Vidor looks through a reducing angle finder to determine camera angles he will use after set is built. Scale models of sets are built to enable the director to plan his shots in advance.

13. Scene from *Hallelujah* showing effect produced when low spot lights are used to project shadows on a background wall.

12. *At left:* Outdoor lighting rig for daytime use. King Vidor is seated on upper platform at left, between megaphone and stool.

14. Daylight was the primary light source on the open stages of the silent era. Natural light filters through the overhead diffusers onto set for *Show People* and a silvered reflector (at right) adds more light to stage area with electric lamps augmenting the natural lighting. The effect produced is flat and two-dimensional.

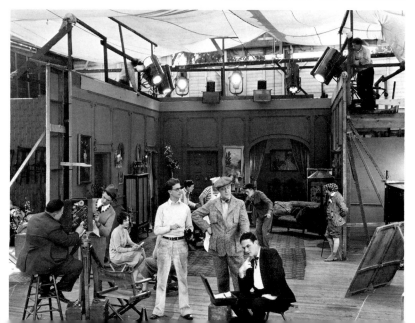

15. Shot from *The Fountainhead* shows use of soft indirect lighting of Patricia Neal and harsh dramatic lighting of Gary Cooper's face. Manhattan skyline in background is actually an enlarged photograph, illuminated from behind.

16. Technical crew with indoor lighting rig are shooting a scene from *Our Daily Bread*. In addition to the camera, overhead spots, arc lamps, and sound booms can be seen.

17. The dedicated silent film star, Lillian Gish, prepared for her death scene in *La Bohème* by not drinking any liquids and sleeping with cotton pads in her mouth for three days before it was filmed.

18. Vidor arranged the warriors in this formation for a scene in *Solomon and Sheba* in order to create the illusion of great depth. Also note the white rope on the ground which shows each extra exactly where to stand. *Photo: Leo Fuchs.*

19. The movement and pacing of the ditchdiggers sequence in *Our Daily Bread* was "choreographed" to strict rhythmic tempos in order to heighten its emotional impact.

20. The single, ingeniously designed set used in *Street Scene* in which the principal house was duplicated at either end of the half-block-long structure: difficult set-ups could be prepared at one house while shooting continued at the other. 21. *Below:* King Vidor on the same set.

22. Pontoon bridge (for *War and Peace*) was built in two hours by the Italian army.

23. Vidor talks with coal miners while on location to film *The Citadel*.

24. Schedule board. Principal characters are listed horizontally at left; the black, vertical strips separate each day of production while each of the strips in between indicates where a given scene is to be filmed (interior or exterior location) and which characters are needed. 25. *Below:* The strips of the schedule board can be switched around in order to make the most efficient use of the sets and of each actor's time.

26. Scene from *H. M. Pulham, Esq.* filmed on an interior stage with manufactured snow that could be formed into snowballs and thrown.

27. Snow scene from *War and Peace* shot on location in the Italian Alps. The perspective created by the long column of troops receding into the distance was planned and required bare snow fields to be effective.

28. Painted background helps create proper mood for this battlefront scene.

29. This improvised camera boom was built on location while filming *Northwest Passage* on location in Idaho in order to make an effective shot of soldiers sleeping in trees above the water.

30. A real (though electrically controlled) explosion during a battle scene in *War and Peace* simulates exploding shells. The dirt above the buried charge was sifted to avoid possible injury to the passing foot soldiers.

31. Spencer Tracy upon awakening from night spent in swamp (*Northwest Passage*).

32. Realistic detail—the smoke screen in the background—has been added to this battle scene by the special effects crew. Also note track for camera boom in right foreground.

CHAPTER 6

WAR AND PEACE AND STREET SCENE

■

Just as Victor Fleming had said during one day's preparation of the film, *The Yearling*, "What do you mean saying I didn't contribute anything? Didn't I say 'No' all day?" Saying "No" can be just as creative as saying "Yes."

One example that stands prominently in my memory concerns the staging of the largest battle scene in the Italian-American production of my film *War and Peace*. It was the Battle of Borodino for which I had had months to think about and prepare. The plan that I formulated in my mind was to select a small valley bordered by a ridge of low hills on either side. I knew we would be limited to about five thousand uniformed foot soldiers plus eight hundred mounted cavalrymen. I wanted the valley to be small enough so that the available number of troops would pack it tightly, much in the way battles were fought during the Napoleonic period. I had studied all available paintings of the actual battle and besides the authenticity of my plan I knew this battle style would be visually effective.

To guide us in finding the perfect location, I had a plaster model built so all those concerned in production would know what I was talking about. In the small scale model I had also placed a foreground hill which would

serve as an ideal camera-placement spot for all long shots
of the spectacle and for Pierre (Henry Fonda) to observe
the entire battle. We determined, through liaison with the
Italian army, which was to supply the fifty-eight hundred
men, the limitations as far as transport was concerned
and we concentrated our search within these boundaries.

After devoting several Sundays to the task (we were already in actual production on other parts of the film)
we found the perfect location; a small valley without trees
surrounded by hills not too high, and a foreground ele-
vation of exactly the right height for mounting our cameras. I had our own Italian production staff consult with
the proper officers of the Italian army for their approval
of the location. After going through several higher eche-
lons, approval was given.

Next, I had diagrammatic layouts made on which I
indicated all important camera set-ups. (See photo 11.) I
paid visits to the actual location and staked out these
camera locations by painting key numbers on the wooden
stakes to correspond with those designated on the printed
layout. In addition I indicated the placement of the various groups of the two contending armies.

In planning the Battle of Borodino I had decided
against the usual practice of letting a second unit director
do the battle scenes while the first director continued to
work with the important members of the cast. Ordinarily,
the battle scenes would be done either before or after the
cast was on salary without building up the daily overhead.
But because of summer maneuvers, or something of the
sort, the Italian army was adamant as to the dates they had
chosen to let us have the troops. These dates occurred
right in the middle of our regular production schedule.

I therefore decided to let Mario Soldati, an Italian
novelist and film director in his own right, take over a
series of scenes using members of the cast while I directed

the Battle of Borodino using only Henry Fonda from the cast of principals. Soldati had been working with me on the script and was familiar with my objectives.

Someone once asked me if I would rather direct a battle scene with 6,000 soldiers or a love scene with two important stars. Without hesitating I answered, "The battle scene." Soldiers don't talk back to you or say they cannot read a certain speech the way it is written. They perform the action the way they are told without trying to preserve or exhibit their personal egos. I had also learned that with proper preparation I could shoot large battle scenes as fast, if not faster, than I could scenes involving two famous stars.

Therefore, for weeks previous to the shooting, I had written out every possible instruction and detail and had each item translated into Italian with multiple copies struck off so that no one involved could plead ignorance. There is no public address system large enough to shout instructions to 800 cavalry and 5,000 foot soldiers while 90 cannon and 2,000 explosions hammer away. There are probably a few egotistically inclined directors who have tried it but I shudder to think of the preponderous confusion they must have created, not to mention the likely result, that what showed on the screen made little sense.

All was in readiness to start shooting the Battle of Borodino on the coming Monday. On Thursday morning the Italian producer of the film came to me on the studio set with the news that the army had changed its mind and rejected the location I had chosen. It would only cooperate if I selected a location on a cavalry post, one hour from Rome in another direction.

In view of the careful preparations, the shortness of time to select and prepare another suitable location, I should have grabbed the closest loudspeaker and yelled "No! No! No!" as loudly and as furiously as I could. The

Italian producer and army officers would have understood that. But I didn't. I was in the midst of doing an important scene with Audrey Hepburn and my first impulse was to be cooperative. What was to be gained by being otherwise? Before long I was to learn a lesson that I would never forget.

On Sunday I started to search for a new battleground within the confines of the area designated by the army. When I found it difficult to duplicate the previous topography I began to feel the pressure of the 7:30 Monday morning call creeping up on me. I started thinking in terms of compromise.

The confines of the cavalry post just didn't have any small valleys with a foreground hill for the cameras and a place of viewpoint for the character of Pierre to observe the battle at the start of the scene. With the enthusiastic approval of the producer, the chief photographer and the production manager (who was only concerned with getting everyone there on time) I settled on a large valley. This valley had a topography similar to the first and for a while I thought it might give an added scope to the battle. Had we had 50,000 troops instead of 5,000, it would have.

We had brought forty extras with us to walk through the specific movement of each contingent of the armies. Stakes were put in the ground and those company commanders who were present knew that they had only to move their men from one designated point to another.

About six or seven small, frail shacks were constructed to be set ablaze during the scenes and three rounds of 2,000 controlled explosions planted in the ground. These controlled explosions, representing exploding shells, are made by planting a black powder mixture about one foot underground. The dirt that is put back into the hole must be sifted through a wire screen so that all solid objects such as pebbles and pieces of branches are sieved out.

Wires from each plant or group of plants are run underground back to a vantage point near the cameras and the director. The explosive areas are marked off on a blueprint and electrically set off from a control board. In this way the special effects technician is theoretically able to time the shell bursts just before or after the advancing soldiers pass. I say theoretically because usually during the shooting of the actual scene a sense of excitement prevails and some plants go off amidst the men. Also, over the location of each explosive charge a red card was placed with the word BOMBA in large type. Each company commander instructed his men to avoid passing directly over these clearly designated spots. In spite of these warnings I saw men step on the Bomba cards as they moved along. In a few instances—while filling in with closer angles—in spite of all precautions I saw a charge detonated while a soldier was directly over it but because the covering earth had been sifted and was not packed tightly over the explosive the man kept right on walking without injury. A few brighter ones, in the same situation but more alert to what was happening, feigned injury or death.

I used this technique extensively throughout the battle scenes of *The Big Parade* and *War and Peace* and I have yet to see any of the participants suffer the slightest injury. (See photo 30.)

Monday morning, up at 6 o'clock. Leave for location at 6:30 to be there by 7:30 for last minute checks and decisions. But before leaving pick three flowers from the garden of my home on the Appia Antica. Make certain that the flowers never get out of my sight until the first scene is in the bag.

Let me explain: Tolstoy's Pierre, a philosophical character, has said in a previous scene that he was going to Borodino as an observer in order to study men under the pressure of battle and impending death. It was not in the book nor written into the script but I had thought that it would be an interesting opening for the battle if Henry Fonda saw a lone flower and was in the process of picking it when he heard the first cannon blast.

Let me inject a word here about the function of the property man with an Italian production unit. It may have changed since, but in 1955–56 there wasn't any such animal. Here we were making a film with ninety-five speaking parts, with a script two and one-half times as long as the ordinary full-length feature screenplay and no property man. When the American production coordinator came to me one day before production began with the startling news that we were to have no property man I refused to get excited and countered with this answer: "The Italians have made some pretty big spectaculars in the past, let's see how they have done them without a prop man. Maybe we have something to learn."

The production assistant didn't appear to relish my stoicism and walked away, convinced that I was even nuttier than he had at first suspected.

This is how the Italians worked it: All properties required on the set during production came under the responsibility of the head set dresser. The trouble with the system is that most of the time he is preparing the sets or locations for subsequent shooting and, therefore, must constantly delegate the responsibility for having the proper article available on the set at the proper moment to one of his underlings. These men were not imbued with the wonderful forethought, ingenuity, and resourcefulness of the typically Hollywood-trained property master.

In approaching the first day's shooting of the Battle of Borodino I visualized the following situation:

Assistant Director: We are all ready, Mr. Vidor, the 6,000 soldiers and cavalry are all costumed and in their places. The 2,000 explosions are ready to go, the 90 cannons are loaded and waiting for the torch as are the six houses to be set on fire. The five technicolor cameras are loaded and the chief sound man says he is ready to roll.

Director: Where is the flower Mr. Fonda is picking when he hears the first sound of battle.

Assistant Director: What flower?

Director: Last Thursday I told Giuseppe Martinelli, the head set dresser, that I would need a flower for the opening scene of the battle.

Assistant Director: Martinelli is back at the studio dressing the sets for next week's shooting.

Director: But he must have told one of his men that I wanted a flower for the opening shot.

Assistant Director: But which one of them? There are at least 20 of his men out here today and they are spread all over the place passing out rifles, lances, first-aid kits, fuses, etc. Which one shall I ask about the flower?

Director: I don't know. Ask them all.

I was determined that the foregoing scene would not take place. So, I picked the flowers myself and I would hold at least one of them in my fingers until I had made an okay take of the opening scene. On the way out to location inside my car I noticed a small glass vase with some water in it. I put two of the three flowers in this vase and told my Italian chauffeur to guard them with his life.

The car delivered me to the raised platform which held the two main cameras and as I watched preparations for the opening scene I unconsciously took occasional sniffs of the small flower I held between the thumb and first finger of my left hand.

(A few days later two Roman newspapers had photographs of me on their first pages with captions reading, "Eccentric American director sniffs yellow carnation while directing huge battle scene.")

Preparations progressed. It is no simple job to clothe nearly 6,000 soldiers in the period costumes and accoutrements of French and Russian fighting men of 1800, but all went smoothly because of the natural efficiency of army methods. Suddenly, I heard a loud voice giving an emphatic order to a driver of one of the automobiles standing by. He was telling him to return to Rome and pick up some important person and bring him to the set. By the time I was able to get an English translation of the order, I realized that *my* chauffeur was getting into *my* automobile and driving away with the two reserve flowers I had picked at 6:30 that morning.

I grabbed the loud speaker and shouted "Stop that car!" A translating assistant leaned over and shouted the message in Italian. Di Laurentiis, the producer, ran to the platform demanding the reason I objected to my automobile being used for an important mission. I said I didn't mind him using my car and driver but I first wanted a vase containing two flowers removed from the car and given to me.

As the two flowers were handed up to me to join the single one I still held between thumb and forefinger, I saw him make a gesture that seemed to say "I suppose all top directors have to be strange in the head." He ended the circular movement of his finger with a typical shrug of the shoulders.

I decided early in my career to keep the direction in which any individual or group is moving consistent and simple. This is especially important in long shots of battles. In fact, it is the only way an army can be identified in a long shot. In close shots it could be assumed that each army would be recognized by their uniforms, but even this form of identification is asking too much of an audience. There is such a conglomeration of uniforms between regiments and battalions that even those in the production crew who spend days on the set with the costumes are often confused.

In the case of *War and Peace* I had decided that all movement of Napoleon's forces on their march toward Moscow would progress from left to right. In this way one could not only easily identify the army by the direction in which it moved, but also *sense* their geographical relationship. (It follows that any group of soldiers moving from right to left would therefore be Russians.) I would never once vary these progressions, believing that the visualization of conflict could only be realized in this manner.

This consistency of direction was an accepted practice in silent films when it came to moving actors in and out of scenes, doorways, and sets. If two characters who were supposed to be looking at each other both looked camera right, even though from a geographical standpoint they were facing each other, the audience would be confused. Script girls were meticulous in their notes regarding camera directions and were quick to remind us if we strayed from this procedure.

In the early days I developed a foolproof method of keeping these directions straight. If I shot a close scene in which John looked camera left, when I selected a spot for Mary who must look camera right I would simply keep my left hand partially folded before me at waist level—the fingers indicating the proper viewpoint. Using this simple trick I could turn in any direction and still be correct. If I made the mistake of having Mary look camera left, the same direction John had looked, it would register that

Mary was interested in someone else but not John. Such was the two-dimensional world in which we lived in the days of silent films.

I am of the opinion that this simplicity and consistency of direction had never been used throughout an entire film until I made *The Big Parade* (1925).

Generally when one looks at a map North is at the top, East to the right, West to the left. Therefore, an American doughboy going from the U.S. to the German-French battlefront would travel from West to East, or left to right. When the war was over he would start retracing his steps in a happier mood moving right to left and continue in that direction across the U.S. if he lived in California or Hawaii. Thus Napoleon's march from Paris to Moscow calls for a left to right progression. In this case any right to left movement would spell retreat, in other words, Napoleon's defeat at the hands of the Russian winter.

As to the recent disregard for consistency of viewpoint shown by some film makers in recent years, I won't say they are wrong. I can't say any creative person is wrong. Wrong is a word that belongs to a church, not a work of art. But I do say that because the motion picture screen is a two-dimensional structure, the film maker, who produces something to show upon it, must be aware of the characteristics of his medium. Why should a director be aware of the relative position of his people and not be able to convey that concept to an audience? Does the presentation of confusion rather than clarity increase the impact of your film or serve to proliferate the bewilderment so many films fall heir to?

In any event, here is the way I laid out the opening shot of the Battle of Borodino which had been one of the major confrontations on Napoleon's march on Moscow. It took place near the village of Borodino which is only a short distance southwest of Moscow. There had been

220,000 troops engaged. Napoleon's forces turned back the Russian resistance under Marshall Kutuzov and the French march towards Moscow continued.

Pierre would be seen scrambling up an embankment to avoid being run down by a galloping troop of Russian cavalry. At the top of the bank, as he paused to catch his breath, his attention would become focused on a yellow flower. As he reached out to pick the flower he would hear the boom of the first cannon. Rising to his feet he would move in the direction of the cannon shot, the camera panning with him. As he reached the brow of the hill he would see Kutuzov's Russian forces moving en masse down the slopes of the hills to the right. This sudden revelation of one part of the battle from Pierre's viewpoint would also be the camera's first view.

Fonda would pause at this position for about eight seconds then move on to position number two. Here he would be able to observe all the activity on the valley floor. After a stop here of precisely ten seconds, he would move on to position number three. At this point, the French army could be seen on the hill slopes to the left massing their forces for the attack. On the skyline of these hills a long line of French cannons were to be already in the process of firing and reloading.

Fonda would pause here for another twelve seconds at which time he would start to move down the slope in order to become more intimately involved with the battle. Cut! End of scene.

Let's go back to the beginning. Here was the problem. Suppose when Fonda was ready to start the scene by crawling up the bank I had called "Camera! Action!" in the usual manner and the same had been relayed over the 50 odd walkie-talkie sets to all commanding officers and the special effects crew had lighted their fires and started their ground explosions. By the time Fonda would have arrived at positions one, two, and three the heat of the scene would have been dissipated.

Also, suppose when Fonda stopped at position number one he had missed his exact mark thereby either covering too much of the background action or excluding it altogether. Could I then yell "Cut" and could the explosive experts stop their fires and explosions? They had prepared their equipment for only three takes which might be necessary because of camera difficulties or light changes, but not because of an actor missing his mark.

This is the way I rehearsed the scene on the previous day and this is the way we shot it:

I give an arm signal to start the cameras rolling

I get an okay sign from each camera operator

I point to a special effects man who fires an aerial bomb which can be plainly heard throughout the valley, alerting all troops. Italian script girl presses stop-watch at sound of bomb and starts counting seconds in Italian over army radio. "Action!"

Time
Elapsed
in Seconds Action

0	Fonda crawls up the embankment.
7	Fonda sees flower and picks it.
12	He hears first cannon fired, rises and starts toward battle.
15	Off camera Russian army starts moving from staked-out point A so that it will be in motion when camera pans to disclose it.
20	Fonda arrives at position one. Russians in action in background. [To avoid any mistake in Fonda's position, we had placed small wooden stakes as markers leaving about two inches

projecting above ground. Fonda was able to feel with the side of his foot whether he had stopped on the exact spot and if not, he could correct his position.]

23   The Russian cavalry goes into action on the floor of the valley.

28   Fonda moves on.

32   Fonda arrives at position two. [At this point, one camera using a telephoto lens moves from Fonda's head and shoulders to a close-up of his hand with the yellow flower. With the massive battle action serving as a backdrop, Fonda releases his hold on the flower and it falls into the dust.]

35   Start action of all French forces on left hillside. Start action of all French artillery.

42   Fonda leaves position two.

47   Arrives at position three, watches advance of Napoleon's army, and firing and reloading of cannons.

59   Fonda starts down slope of hills for closer observation of battle.

75   Cut! Stop the cameras. Stop the battle. Get ready for Take 2.

Everything had worked perfectly but we had shot the first take with an overcast sky as a protection in the event the weather worsened. I was worried lest the 2,000 troops farthest from the camera would not register on the screen. I checked with Cardiff, the chief photographer. He thought they would be seen. As insurance he wanted to paint a mass of troops on a plate glass he had rigged before one of his cameras. How long would this take? He said he could be ready as soon as the army was regrouped for Take 2. The sun was beginning to come out more clearly. I thought the brightness would help define the 2,000 to 2,500 soldiers lost in the bigness of the valley.

Take 2 was in the bag by 10:30 A.M., but I was to learn later that neither the chief photographer's glasspainting (I should explain here that Cardiff was a first-class painter in oils—otherwise the whole idea would have been preposterous) nor the bright sunlight brought the troops farthest from camera into useful definition. This fault could have been avoided had I said "No" at the appropriate time.

Then we moved with Pierre into the heat of the battle. No spectator ever became more intimately involved in the fighting. Finally Napoleon, sensing the battle going against him, sends in his cavalry reserves to stem the tide. We had some wonderful horse and rider falls in this attack. I have been asked many times how they were done.

In early Hollywood Westerns a rig called a "flying W" was used to catapult a horse and rider into a running spill. Then the Society for the Prevention of Cruelty to Animals began to take notice and the practice was outlawed. From then on horses were taught to fall upon command of the rider. These were given by signals from the reins and knees. Soft ground is usually prepared at the point of fall and rocks and pieces of wood removed.

In Italy a quite different technique has been developed. A pit of approximately seven feet long by four feet wide by three feet deep is dug. The surface opening is then covered by a paper-base composition board which is spread with a thin layer of dirt to cover the whiteness of the board. On the far side of the pit the soil is sifted and all articles that might cut horse or rider are removed. Just before the scene is shot this ground on the far side of the pit receives a good sprinkling of water so that the horse and rider upon hitting it in a fall will slide to a stop rather than halt abruptly which could well cause serious injury.

The horse falls in *War and Peace* were the most spectacular I have ever seen and not once was the composition board exposed nor could it be seen that the horse's front legs were going into a pit. About a dozen of these falls, executed at full gallop, were made in the cavalry charge and I saw no horse or rider injured. When the picture first showed in the U.S., I was able to sign a paper to this effect at the request of the S.P.C.A. It is interesting to see how impressive these falls are and yet, because of careful preparation, how humane.

A later scene called for the cavalry with lances drawn to charge a line of fortresses by jumping the dirt barriers and landing amongst firing cannons and busy artillerymen. As a safety measure my American production assistant had ordered 500 rubber-tipped spears. We were getting ready to make the scene when the production assistant came to me in terrible anguish saying that he had been double-crossed by the Italian production chief and we could not make the scene. He had in his hand one of the spears with its sharp hardwood point which could go through a man just about as easily as a metal one could. He was followed closely by the Italian production chief with excuses as to why the rubber manufacturer could not produce the rubber tips in time and other reasons which failed to ring true. In a moment it looked as if the two men were coming to blows. It immediately struck me that this was a most inappropriate time and place for a personal battle. I grabbed the arm of the American as he was about to swing and pulled him to one side. I told him that he had done everything that he should and could do in the line of safety, that the Italians had chosen to reject his caution and now the responsibility was *theirs,* not *ours.* My argument prevailed and calmed him down. Still, as director of the scene, I felt a large responsibility to all those participating in it and I had to do everything I could to protect them. As I have said somewhere else, there is no such thing as an audience opinion, only the opinion of a group of individuals, so I decided to put our problem directly in the hands of each individual combatant.

We asked all the cavalrymen to dismount and artillery-men in the fortresses to come to a position before our camera set-up. I told them about the order for the rubber tipped spears and tactfully said that they had not arrived in time. I told them that the scene must look real and effective but not at the cost of anyone getting hurt. I said it was in the hands of each individual to see that no one got stabbed by a wooden spear. I tried to pave the way for intelligence and reason to prevail.

It worked. In two takes of a very exciting and potentially dangerous scene only one participant received an injury and this was a minor surface cut on his leg caused by an unruly mount. A small casualty list, indeed, for a scene this hazardous.

During lunch that day someone asked me if, while directing a large battle scene, I ever felt like Napoleon. "Napoleon?" I replied, "Hell, Napoleon could only direct one side of a battle."

The script called for a pistol duel between Pierre and Dolokhov set on a snowy hill at sunrise. There were no snowy hills close to Rome at the time. One possibility was to journey north to the Italian Alps and find one. Let's say that on location we would have to get up in the middle of the night to have all cameras, actors, and equipment ready in time to start shooting as the sun appeared on the horizon. But the scene was to take two days to complete and where would the sun and the long shadows be as the sun climbed to its apex? Duels with the sun directly overhead just aren't dramatic.

We decided on Stage 6, the largest stage of the Cine-Citta studio. A chemical company at Monte Cattini had perfected a mixture that came out of a flexible tube and looked like shaving cream. Given ten or fifteen minutes to dry and harden it formed a shiny crust that was ideal for a Russian duel scene shot at sunrise.

Now we had to make time stand still and hold the sun at the horizon for two days. I have said before that Jack Cardiff, in addition to being a fine photographer, was an experienced and first-class oil painter. He set up his frame of clear glass about three feet in front of the camera, placed a baby spotlight alongside and slightly behind the camera and put a faint diffusion disk over the lamp lens. After a few moments of adjustment he asked me to look through the camera. Presto! There by reflection in the glass was our hazy sunrise sun right on the horizon where it remained for two days.

The long shadows of the actors and the bright shiney surface of the snow was created by a high-intensity lamp called a "Brute" placed above the wintery cyclorama background and just out of camera range.

Much more comfortable to make snowy dawn scenes in a well controlled stage than on an Alp at zero plus 10— except for one difficulty. The chemical mixture, when one spent much time near it, caused nose and eyes to water profusely. We kept the actors out in the sunlight until the last minute of preparation. In this way their faces were kept dry and the audience didn't have to figure out whether they were weeping for themselves or the other fellow.

We had a pretty good budget allowance, five or six million, depending on whose books you examined. Not bad for two wealthy countries in a capitalist economy but very late in the shooting, production money ran out. I had only one absolutely necessary scene yet to do and when I was told by the Italian head of production to eliminate it, this time I said "NO" in no uncertain terms. But they still held the (empty) purse strings.

Early in the production we had made scenes of Audrey

Hepburn with her cousin Sonia and her father in a box of the Moscow Opera House supposedly during a performance of an opera. In this scene she meets Anatole Kuragin for the first time. Before Anatole visited her box she had engaged in a mild flirtation while he was seated in the regular seats, or stalls, as they are called in England.

Originally, when Audrey and Mai Britt were on salary, we had planned to use the Rome Opera House as a stand-in for its comrade in Moscow but at that time they were renovating it. To keep from carrying certain members of the cast on salary for a long period of extra time we built two full boxes, complete with red velvet and gold, in the studio.

This now becomes a little study in how to shoot scenes in crowded opera house of a large city without the necessary finances. You can beg a ham sandwich from a neighbor but where can you beg an opera house full of formally dressed Moscovites in the period of 1800?

The officials of the Italian company kept sending me around central Italy on a wild goose chase hoping I'd find an opera house (*gratis*) that could double for Moscow. The Rome Opera House was now available for a fee of $1,000 but the company didn't have the necessary wherewithal. They didn't tell me that this was the problem until later. What good would it have done in the first place if they didn't have the money?

As a last resort I turned to all my early experience and accumulated know-how, to figure out a way to get the needed scenes onto VistaVision, Technicolor film. I located the drapery department of the inactive studio and found many rolls of moth-eaten red velvet on the shelves.

With the help of a few loyal assistants we pulled these out and hung them on one wall of an empty stage. Then we put a row of idle four-foot camera platforms (in studio parlance, "parallels") along the base of the wall. Along these platforms, with the help of an idle electrician, we strung a row of lamps to serve as footlights. We only had to lift the next row of red velvet about ten inches to cover the lamps and the platforms. Behold, an opera stage with footlights, before the curtain rises, of course. A few nights before I had visited the Rome Opera House as an afficianado and I had observed that when the overture began all you could see of the orchestra was the head and shoulders of the conductor and the top part of the neck of a bass fiddle. The sound of a large orchestra enabled the audience to take the rest for granted.

This was easy. Another row of red velvet strung on two-by-fours, a low stool to keep the "Maestro" from projecting up too high, a broken neck of a bass instrument from the prop room, a portable phonograph brought from my home and presto—an orchestra pit with a full symphony orchestra, at least when the musical scoring of the picture was completed for which there was still an allotment in the budget.

The company came through with a maximum of twenty extras dressed in whatever costumes they could find in the idle wardrobe department. I appointed one extra as the orchestra conductor (all Italians can wave their arms in time to a phonograph); I put Vittorio Gassman in the midst of them for his flirtatious moments with Natasha while the footlights came up in the background as the Maestro mounted his podium and raised his baton for the overture to begin.

Oh yes—about the long shot of the packed auditorium. Before actual photography on the picture had begun, I had gone to Milan specifically to hear Maria Callas in a performance of *La Traviata*. I had brought back a large colored photograph of the interior of La Scala taken during some very special occasion. I studied the photograph and speculated how much movement it would take to simulate a live audience.

The company still had a credit account with the Technicolor Laboratories in London because the negative of the film was held by them so they knew they would be paid. Also, I knew they had a good special effects department. I sent my souvenir photograph of La Scala to them, requested them to more or less duplicate it as a somewhat larger-sized painting and to attach tiny pieces of tinfoil to about a dozen spots on the painting. When the painting was photographed they would please set up a small electric fan nearby with the hope that the fluttering pieces would seem as if some opera devotees were fanning themselves while the overture was being played. I added that if they had trouble finding a light tinfoil, I knew that Selfridge's Department Store on Oxford Street sold Wrigley's Doublemint Gum.

The first few times the Italian-American production of *War and Peace* was shown, I always singled out someone to ask what they thought of the Moscow Opera House sequence. The answer invariably was, "Where on earth did you shoot that? And all those people! Must have cost a pretty penny."

It is ironic that even on my most expensive and elaborate film containing so much on-location footage (and it is, I believe, one of my best), a depleted budget should have forced me to draw on the ingenuity and resourcefulness that were absolutely necessary for survival in the old studio days—speaking of which, another production comes to mind.

I remember my approach to the job of making a film of the one-set play *Street Scene* (1931). The play took place in front of a New York City tenement house of four floors. I considered the possibility of going inside some of the flats and of going to other exterior locations in order to inject some kind of action into the film. While I was pondering this possibility, a fortunate thing happened. On the studio lot, I passed a workman sleeping out part of his lunch hour and I noticed that a very active fly roamed about his face without awakening him. The fly seemed most interested in all the hills and valleys of the workman's face. The thought struck me that, to a camera lens, the variety of details of the front, sidewalk, and street of a tenement building can be unlimited. Through everchanging camera set-ups, through carefully planned composition and design, the film could have much more actual movement than with the conventional set-up of a camera at eye level in a western film with stage coaches, cowboys, and indians galloping by ad infinitum.

Working in close cooperation with the cinematographer and the set designer, we indicated each camera set-up on a series of duplicate prints of the single set. I had decided to avoid repeating the same camera set-up twice. Where the play had been confined to the facade of the building and the sidewalk before it, I could, without destroying the purity of the playwright's concept, pull back and also utilize the street in front of the building. After all, the play was called *Street Scene*. This treatment proved most effective in preserving the visual and dramatic impact of the play, without any artificial injection of movement.

Another interesting technical trick that was used in this film can be noted here. Most of the entrances and exits of the characters in the play showed them approaching or leaving along the sidewalk requiring us to shoot in both directions from the principal house. Had we put our house in the center of the street it would have meant constructing a full New York City block. Instead we were able to build only half a city block. By putting a duplicate main house at each end we could, by utilizing the proper house for shooting each direction, show a half block beyond. The duplicate house at the end of the half block was too far from the camera to be detected. Having two duplicate houses also enabled us to prepare difficult set-ups at one while shooting was progressing at the other. For instance, a platform outside a third story window would be installed with camera and lights without delaying the work of the main production unit.

The entire half-block-long structure and street with elevated railway station at one end was all covered with a network of wires so that light-colored diffusers could be used to eliminate direct sunlight when a diffused effect was needed. Above the white shade was arranged heavier black material which eliminated a large percentage of all daylight when the subject was to be lighted artificially. I suppose the earlier experience with sunlight control on open air stages paid off in the making of this film. (See photos 20 and 21.)

One of the greatest obstacles in Hollywood production is the impracticability of having a thorough production rehearsal period with all the members of the cast. As you know the Guild forbids actors appearing for rehearsal unless they are carried through on salary until their part begins in the film. However, in the making of *Street Scene,* because the setting for the entire film was available as were all members of the cast, I was able to rehearse for one week prior to production. This made it possible to complete the film in twenty-four shooting days. The actors were available because they all began work on the first two days of shooting and there was no need to compensate anyone for idle time.

II THEORY AND TECHNIQUE: *The Elements of Cinema*

▣

CHAPTER 7

DEVELOPING VISUAL
AWARENESS

■

We are dealing here with a visual and, to a lesser extent, aural medium. I am convinced that the visual component is ten times—perhaps even a hundred times—more important to the total impact of a film than the aural. One of the most puzzling awards each year is the Academy Award for perfection in sound recording. In watching a film unreel have you ever spontaneously remarked, "What good sound recording?" Where musical scoring is concerned, you'll probably answer yes, but good sound recording is usually taken for granted; if not up to standard it should be corrected. I believe the same is more or less true of editing. I have often wondered how the members of the film editors branch of the Academy decide on the best editing job done by one of their colleagues. It would seem that the evaluators would have to know what footage and how many options had been supplied by the director to the editor before they could make a fair judgment of the editor's accomplishment.

In preparing to become a maker of films, the novice must learn to think visually, think visually, think visually —not only with a camera in his hands, but with his entire consciousness.

I have often wondered why I am compelled to read every roadside billboard, every license plate on each car I am following. Every tree, every field, every barn, every house must come under my graphic scrutiny. I am a Camera. It came about naturally, I wanted it that way. There are so many tell-tale landmarks on each route I take that I seldom need directions if I have to repeat the drive. In fact, there can be so many points of visual identification in a route I have never traveled before that I very often arrive at a predetermined destination without having received specific directions.

What I am saying is, "Look, watch, observe, remember, and record." After a while, it will become automatic. You will be able to find your way around—and you will be able to find your way around in movie making.

When I was in my teens and had a job as ticket-taker in a local nickelodeon working a twelve-hour shift from 10 A.M. to 10 P.M., I became intrigued with the pantomimic gestures of the silent film actors. The comedians of the French cinema seemed more adept. These were followed closely by the actors under the direction of D. W. Griffith and the members of Mack Sennett's group of comedians. One soon learned that certain gestures had specific meanings. Some could express a verbal sentence or paragraph with such fullness and brevity that they must be classified as cinema art. Gestures, body movement, and facial expression were our only language. This means of expression so prevailed among film makers that they often detailed scenes to producers and actors in terms of pantomine or by using the gestures themselves.

The language of gestures has continued to fascinate me ever since. I invented a little game which I play at every opportunity. On the street whenever I see two people carrying on an animated conversation and I happen to be too far away to hear the gist of what they are saying, I experiment with dialogue that would fit their gestures.

Usually when this occurs, I am at the wheel of an automobile and the talkers are close enough for me to see their expressions as an aid in concocting my scene. On occasion, I have gotten out of the car and walked by in the hope of hearing enough to check the accuracy of my improvisation.

In silent films, the visual component was definitely and obviously predominant, embellished of course by the accompaniment of a large orchestra or an expressive Wurlitzer organ. Let us consider for a moment what percentage of our total enjoyment of the film this musical accompaniment represents and we would probably agree on one-third or one-quarter. Now weigh this figure against the participation percentage of today's complete dialogue and music sound track. The disparity between them may seem surprising if you haven't made the comparison before.

Those few directors who boast that photography does not interest them cannot in my opinion be referred to as "auteurs," which is an explicit term. Of course, the meaning of the word in French is "author" but with a broader meaning than its English equivalent. Its connotations include much more than simply the authorship of original, written material. It means the control of screenplay, casting, decor, editing, acting, with a dynamic emphasis on the supervision of photography.

We should become increasingly aware of the elements that distinguish an interesting film from a dull one. Of course, visual awareness on the part of the film maker is a crucial factor. This is the dough that makes the bread. (Whether it is Russian rye, French or, whole wheat is another question, one that involves the director's use of style and subject matter, and it also plays a big role in the total impact of the film.)

I have said before that the story cannot be wholly depended upon to make that great film. What then? Is there one ingredient that can do the trick? Or, is it a combination of all the elements or the majority of them?

The first films that come to mind when I ask myself this question are:

> Fellini's *La Dolce Vita* and 8½.
> Antonioni's *Blow-Up.*
> Mike Nichols' *The Graduate.*
> Fred Zinneman's *Man For All Seasons.*
> George Stevens' *Shane.*
> David Lean's *Brief Encounter, The Bridge on the River Kwai,* and *Lawrence of Arabia*
> More recently, Robert Rafelson's *Five Easy Pieces.*

All these films had moderately adequate stories, none were formidable from a literary point of view. All were photographed with first-class craftsmanship (*Lawrence of Arabia* being the only outstanding one in this department). All were directed, edited, acted, scored, costumed, located, sound-tracked according to highly developed standards. What then? What was the x-factor that impressed me sufficiently to cause me to remember them here?

I believe they all exhibited some facet of the film maker's character—more precisely his individuality, his sensibility or his unconscious, if you like—that caused the actors to act as they did, that caused the photographer to put his camera where he did, that guided the screenplay to take the course that it did and the film editor to edit as he did.

Nichols was a successful performing comedian utilizing sophisticated material before he turned director. Fellini's best films are all self-analytical, Zinnerman is a quiet, gentle man at heart, Stevens is determined, deliberate. I have not spent enough time with David Lean to know what actually goes on underneath but I can detect evidences of it in each scene he directs.

For our benefit, I want to speak in terms of specifics. Intangibles are not acceptable when one takes his place beside the camera. Here are some other films that made a lasting impression on me:

Claude LeLouch's *A Man and a Woman.*
Elia Kazan's *On the Waterfront*
Kurosawa's *Rashomon*
Ingmar Bergman's *Wild Strawberries* and *Virgin Spring*

What moments in these films made a lasting imprint on my memory? In *A Man and a Woman,* I remember the reflection of moving trees on the windshield as the couple drove along a French country road, and an apparently unrehearsed scene in a railway station restaurant. But these are only two scenes of a complete film. What does this indicate?

Kazan's *On the Waterfront:* A powerful scene on the rear seat of an automobile between Marlon Brando and Rod Steiger.

Rashomon: A shot of a lovely Japanese wife as she moves along on horseback, her intense eyes peering out from the shadows of a white veil suspended from a wide-brimmed hat.

Wild Strawberries: Bergman, through the skillful integration of religious and metaphysical symbols into the story of one day in a man's life, managed to transcend the conventional boundaries of time and transport his viewers into the limitless vistas of consciousness.

Virgin Spring: The rage expressed in the tearing down of a lone sapling on a hilltop. The rape of the young girl done with taste and distinction. I feel that with all the means and angles of fornication that have been projected since, no one has equalled Bergman's treatment.

Don't think for a minute that I remember these films because of one or two scenes. They serve as keys to the whole concept and execution of each. There was a period when I felt that an entire film could be evaluated by the opening one or two shots. It may still be true. If the film maker knows what he is doing, he will get to his message immediately. If he is not in control, he will fake around with some pseudo-impressive opening shots that have very little to do with the guts of his subject. Similarly, scenes I remember are indications of the meaning and power of the entire film in which they appeared.

> John Ford's *The Informer* and *Stagecoach*
> (When *Stagecoach* was remade a few years ago without Ford, it came and left, unpraised and unnoticed.)
> *Zorba the Greek* (For friends hovering around a dying woman like so many locusts.)
> Francois Truffaut's *The Four Hundred Blows*.
> George Stevens' *A Place in the Sun*.
> John Huston's *Treasure of the Sierra Madre*
> D. W. Griffith's *Intolerance*.

In each, there are vivid impressions I retain of moments in which I experienced an emotion that transcended the commonplace, when a new door was opened on life, my consciousness expanded. For these experiences I must thank individual man, operating as an artist expressing the universality of all men—his underlying emotional life, his strivings, and his dreams. I must also be grateful that man has been endowed with the great power of visual awareness and the present-day tools to communicate these powers to others.

René Clair's *Le Million* and *Sous les Toits de Paris*
Marcel Pagnol's *Harvest* and *Baker's Wife*

In these last, the impact of the films may also have been due to the Gallic viewpoint of the film maker in addition to being the result of visual power. Pagnol inaugurated a type of dialogue that argued the point under discussion backward and forward, up and down, with a humanness that had not been accomplished before. Still the extremely expressive face of the actor Fernandel seems to have much to do with imprinting certain scenes on my memory. I must here again stress the individuality of the film maker.

In my own film *The Big Parade,* for years after its first showing and until this day, people speak of the moment the doughboy, played by John Gilbert, removes a heavy shoe from a pack on his back and throws it to his French sweetheart as a desperate token of his affection. Equal to this, they speak of the close-up in which the same girl in an impulsive move to slow the truck's progress holds to a chain at the rear of the truck that is carrying her lover to war. The film is a mighty panorama of World War I decidedly in the spectacle category and yet the memory is of two close-ups. A hundred airplanes in a sweep over a battlefield is never mentioned.

For years another scene from one of my films was repeatedly recalled to me by various people who remembered it, but remembered nothing else about the rest of the film, not even the title or leading players. All that was written in the silent picture scenario concerning this scene was: "Love scene here."

I had selected for the setting of the scene a small lake on the outskirts of Los Angeles. En route to the location, I had no idea what the two lovers would be doing on the shore of the lake, but I hoped for an inspiration when I looked at the place, aided by the cinematographer and our "camera

eyes." In the era of silent films, there was no problem involved in improvising a scene on the spot. No dialogue
had to be carefully written and learned, action and pantomime could be invented even after the camera was going.

We looked at the banks of the lake but found them
either muddy or weedy and uninviting. We examined the
surrounding meadow but it was harsh, dry, and rocky
with no wild flowers to wallow in.

Returning to the lake, I suddenly noticed a lone willow
tendril hanging from a tree and caressing the quiet surface
of the water.

I asked the prop man, who, with the assistant director
and the camera operator, was following us about.

"How long do you think it would take to find a boat
that would be historically accurate?" (The story was by
Sabatini and was laid in France in the reign of Louis XIV.)

"How large a boat?" he asked.

"Oh, something like an oversized row boat."

"I heard that we were going to a lake today so I brought
one along."

Prop men at times perform miracles and this was one of
those times. Just like that, he had pulled a period row
boat out of his pocket.

Turning to the assistant, I asked him to see how long it
would take to construct a corridor of weeping willow
branches duplicating precisely the aesthetic effect the lone
branch before us was suggesting. The answer came back
that it could be done in from forty minutes to an hour.

John Gilbert and Eleanor Boardman half recline on
pillows in the bow of the boat—behind them a white
parasol. The camera photographing them rides with them
in the other end of the boat. The boat is propelled slowly
forward while Gilbert caresses with his lips the cheeks of
the lovely Eleanor. The boat's gentle progress causes the
willow branches and leaves to divide as they pass the

camera and swing back into formation directly in front of the camera lens in an out-of-focus kaleidoscopic design in which the lovers are seen only mistily. From the lens, the supple branches and leaves move on to gently caress the bodies, then the faces, even the lips of the lovers. And as if this were not enough, the leaves move on to form light and shadow patterns on the top of the white parasol. The sun was exactly in the right place to help us achieve this effect—God and the M.G.M. camera department working hand in hand. (See photo 3.)

Could the beauty, poetry, and rhythm of this scene have been expressed by any other medium? Does not the final result of this scene exemplify what cinema is all about?

CHAPTER 8

FILM FORM AND THE EDITING PROCESS

■

A motion picture, whatever the length, makes a statement. A statement, whatever the content, should have a
form. A humorous story usually has a surprise finish, or an
unexpected twist at the ending. One of the most usual
forms in the theater is first act, second act, third act,
beginning, middle, and end. This is not to say that there
have not been interesting plays in two acts and occasionally in one act. For a long period, this three act form of
the theater carried over into the movies. Griffith was the
first to break away, but his innovations were just the beginning. In recent years there have been many sincere ef-
forts to get away from the theater form and establish an
original cine form. Recently when someone asked Antonioni if he didn't believe that a film should have a first
act, second act, third act—beginning, middle, and end, he
answered, "Certainly I do, but not necessarily in that
order."

I have always tried to associate my best films with a
musical form, more precisely the symphonic form. This
enabled me to consider the film's structure in terms of
basic theme, counter theme, development or complication
including recurrent theme lines and, finally, a crescendo to
a climax followed by an ending scene or two correspond-
ing to the closing chords of a symphony.

I first became aware of the relationship between musical and film form while viewing the films of D. W. Griffith. At the theater in which they played in Los Angeles a full symphony orchestra was there in the pit. Special musical scores were written as accompaniment for the larger silent films and played by full orchestra alternating with massive Wurlitzer organs. These big films moved from city to city carrying with them a maestro, a top projectionist and a staff for publicity, accounting, and management. This arrangement for certain large scale films was called a "Road Show."

In watching D. W. Griffith's *Intolerance,* I became aware that the horse-drawn chariots were traveling at approximately seventy miles an hour. The mounting excitement of each progressive shot demanded that the chariots appear to be traveling at this speed. I saw that film form had an inherent flexibility rather than being under the control of technical rigidity. The rule was art—not documentation.

In *Intolerance,* Griffith used an extremely imaginative film form, one whose scope has never been equalled to this day. He wanted to show how intolerance operated through the ages. There were four separate stories, each in a different historical setting: the destruction of ancient Babylon by Cyrus and his invaders; the religious persecution of the Huguenots by Catherine de Medici in 16th-century France; a condensed account of the life of Jesus Christ; a contemporary capital and labor story laid in the U.S. These four stories were loosely held together by a scene of Lillian Gish in a rocking chair beside an infant's crib, a symbol of time, eternity, rebirth.

Griffith's idea of film form, as far as this picture was concerned, was to jump back and forth from one story to the other as the emotional impact or dramatic tempo paralleled. As the overall structure progressed toward a climax and the pace increased, the parts used in each episode would become shorter, thereby creating a unified form of pace and rhythm that encompassed the tempo of the individual scene itself.

Intolerance was one of the most imaginative projects ever attempted in film form. It was probably too gigantic for the average public to absorb in one evening. It did not achieve half the success at the box office of Griffith's previous film *The Birth of a Nation*. It was dissected into its basic four parts which were then distributed and sold as four separate feature films. Bosley Crowther in his book *The Great Films* says of Griffith's masterwork *Intolerance,* "In his great burst of power and ostentation Griffith tried to do too many things with too little awareness of the necessity of cohesive form and style." Nevertheless, how many films since *Intolerance* can you think of which are large enough in conception to be separated into four full-length movies?

When I was studying Tolstoy's great novel *War and Peace* in anticipation of starting work on the screenplay, I was thinking very much about film form. There was so much material in the book that couldn't possibly be used in the proposed film that I had to organize a plan that would guide us in the selection of the episodes that could be most successfully adapted. There were so many characters in the book that the edition from which I worked was accompanied by a twelve-page supplement whose purpose was to organize the various members into family groups in such a manner that the story and its episodes would be understandable and digestible to the reader. You can see why I had to establish a pattern, a ground plan, in order to bring all this material into a film script. Then I remembered *Intolerance*. Griffith had held the reins of four stories running concurrently and so could I. But after further study of the book, I realized that this was exactly

the form that Tolstoy had used. A chapter for Natasha,
one for Pierre, then Andrey for a chapter and one for
Nicolas at the front. As the story progresses and the action
quickens, the cuts to the various stories are shorter and
finally they all come together in one major thread. Unlike
Griffith at this point, but very much in the form of a
musical symphonic pattern.

A diagram I made in the pre-production days to help
clarify in my mind the relationship of the principal
characters is reproduced below.

Natasha is the central protagonist about whom the story
revolves. The double lines in Chart 1, like a highway,
show her principle contacts: Nicholas, her brother; Pierre,
her friend; Andrey, her lover. The other lines indicate
lesser contacts and their relationship with either one or
two of the four principal characters. This chart was made,

Chart 1

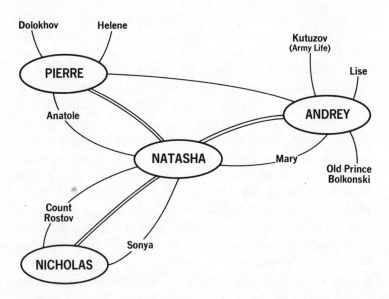

not from the book, but from the screenplay, some time before shooting began. I made it solely for my own use, as a reminder or simplification of the major scenes that would have to be filmed to cover important story points. I wanted to be able to see at a glance whether certain characters affected, or were affected by the lives of other characters.

In the second part of the film, Napoleon enters the picture and sets up a whole new chart of his own, sort of an outside synthesis that imposes an arbitrary force on all the other characters, drastically changing the course of their normal lives. This change, like the effect of an earthquake or a hurricane, is sometimes referred to as *Deus ex machina* that is, an event or character suddenly introduced to resolve a situation or untangle a plot. In *War and Peace,* Napoleon could hardly be called a suddenly introduced device but his entrance into Moscow changed the lives of all the characters in the story. Napoleon's imposition on the form of the screenplay is seen more precisely in *War and Peace* Chart 2 (p. 122), a visual memo on the structure of the original novel.

The *War and Peace* Chart 2 was made in the early days of work on the screenplay and does not necessarily follow the finished film. It shows that the job of adaptation was extremely complicated. I was working from a sixteen-hundred-page novel in two volumes whose filmed counterpart would have to be shown in one evening in the theater.

In *The Citadel* (1938) Dr. Manson, upon completion of his medical training, accepts a meager assignment in a small Welsh mining village. He has dramatic experiences in keeping with the provincialism of the village. The makeup of his character compels him to move on and he finds a more lucrative position in a larger town.

Still more provincial prejudices confront him here which propel his next move to a large city, London.

Chart 2

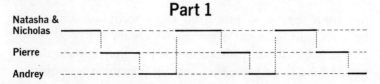

Part 1

Above: The normal domestic lives of the Bolkonsky and Rostov families in the initial chapters of the book.

Below: The catalytic and catastrophic effect of Napoleon's entry into Russia; the inscrutable strategy of General Kutuzov.

Part 2

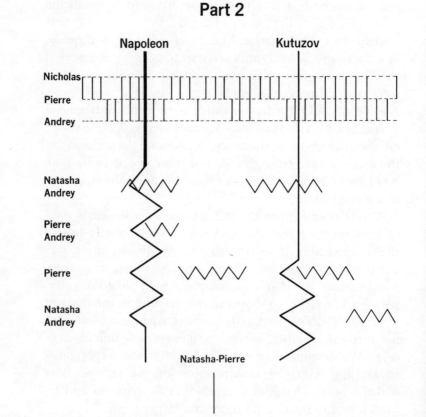

In London, the struggle for survival finally leads to the material success of a secure—albeit hypocritical—practice among London's elite.

The integrity of his true nature soon rebels at the moral corruption inherent in his dishonest position, thereby turning him back to the struggles that were part of his original altruistic goal. One can think of the form of these

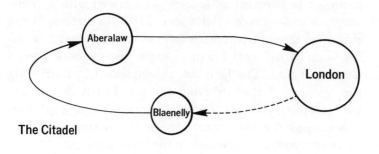

elements as story construction and at one point during the writing of the screenplay I, no doubt, would think of them in this manner. But when it comes near to production, I begin to transform my overall picture into a visual diagram that serves as a useful pattern in my approach to the actual filming.

The stage dramatist thinks in acts, the novelist in chapters, the film maker in sequences. The length of an act is partially related to the length of the other acts but not precisely so. The three-act form arises from the need to establish the situation, further complicate it, and finally untangle it, (the denoument). If this plan is followed, the author must bring all the action together in three time sequences, permitting for slight variations. The novel and film form have more inherent freedom to move about either in time or space. Examine the scope of D. W. Griffith's *Intolerance* which embraced four historic episodes over a time span of several centuries. This is an unusual example but illustrates the unlimited boundaries of cinema form. Another example of breaking the time barrier is Kubrick's *2001*.

A sequence in a film is a unified time element related to an act in the theater, only shorter. In earlier films, each sequence began with a *"fade-in"* and ended with a *"fade-out."* Hand-cranked Bell and Howell cameras were equipped with an automatic fade device that could be set for fades of different lengths ranging from about two to six feet of film. The fade was accomplished by narrowing the opening of the revolving shutter. When the shutter was completely closed, the camera came to a stop. This process put the fade indelibly on the original negative thereby saving a process step in the laboratory.

It began to appear that the fade-in and fade-out were slowing down the progressive tempo and they began to give way to the *dissolve* (or *mix*). However, the fade was still used at the beginning and end of the film and at the beginning and end of a group of sequences that formed a distinct unit or act.

The *dissolve* (originally called the "lap dissolve") had the effect of beginning the next scene while the preceding scene was still on the screen, a sort of welding process whose effectiveness I believed to be greatly exaggerated. In my last films at M.G.M., I tried to inaugurate the use of direct cutting to replace most dissolves but I never completely succeeded in making the change. Previous usage had developed into a studio policy that proved impossible to break.

When a completed film reached the laboratory stage, it came under the supervision of front office editors who were in a position to exercise control over such items. It was presumed that the direct cut did not suggest a time change but in actuality there is more of a separation between two end-to-end scenes than there are in two scenes whose action partially overlap. The fade gave the effect of the lowering and lifting of a curtain, a direct hangover from the proscenium arch, but the dissolve had no such subliminal influence behind it. It was supposed to give the effect of action flowing into the next time sequence.

Griffith at one time experimented with putting an extremely short fade (two to four frames only) at the beginning and end of each scene. This was a daring innovation ignoring the required flexibility for the editing process to follow. It was like holding one's hand in front of the lens and uncovering it at the precise moment when the scene attained a point of dramatic interest. I was making one of my first feature films and when the news reached me about what Griffith was doing, I considered it worth a try. However, after one or two days I abandoned the idea, knowing that the quick fades could not live through the "meticulous" job in the cutting room.

In the early Hollywood years it was customary to use an iris device in front of the lens to affect transitional changes between scenes or sequences. This was a device mounted on brackets in front of the camera lens which could close the scene with a round, contracting circle which concentrated the attention on one spot—usually a face—for a final accent before blocking out the scene completely (*iris-out*). This camera technique worked as well in reverse (*iris-in*) which focused all the attention on an important face or prop, such as a telephone or a revolver before revealing the entire scene. One can readily see the increased dramatic accent an iris-in, or an iris-out could give compared to an over-all fading of a scene.

Later on came the *wipe* in which one scene pushes the

preceding one off the screen in a sideways, sometimes diag-
onal movement. Wipes are still frequently used, principally
with credit titles or in television commercials. It is impractical to make them in the camera. They must be made on a
step printer in a process laboratory so equipped.

It is impossible to set any rules about the number of
sequences in a feature film but going back over some of
my old scripts I would say that the average is from fifty
to seventy.

But before giving any examples from my own work I
should pause to clarify the meaning of the following terms
and how they are related. Individual *shots* (close-ups, long
shots, panning, etc.) are assembled (through cutting) into
coherent *scenes* which in turn are grouped to form *sequences* or episodes. These are ultimately combined in
the final version of the film; how this is done, the relationship between the sequences, is a prime factor in shaping
the over-all *form* of the completed film.

Examining the first scenes of the final script of my film
War and Peace, I find that the first major scene in the first
sequence has 55 separate cuts (or shots); second sequence,
first scene, 48 cuts; second scene, 4 cuts; and the third
scene, 28 cuts.

The second scene with only four cuts is a long walking-
perambulating scene played mainly with dialogue. Other
scenes examined in the film run to 11, 38, and 41 separate
cuts so you see there is no set pattern to go by. This varies
with the type of story, the pace of the action and whether
the director has a light touch or prefers a slower, more
ponderous style.

While shooting a film I usually carry, either in a pocket
or on a clipboard, only the scene or sequence in which I
am involved that day. I use loose-leaf ring binders to hold

the entire script so pages can be easily withdrawn or replaced for daily use.

The short comedies of the Mack Sennett era and later the full length ones of Harold Lloyd and Charlie Chaplin usually finished up with what was called a chase. Its substance was just that, with the comedian using every movie device to escape the determined villains, or the equally determined lawmen. This form gave excitement where it was needed most, when interest was beginning to lag. It served as a mounting climax, a musical crescendo just before the final fade-out.

In discussing film form in my class at the University of Southern California, we measured the running time of different musical compositions as recorded on tapes and discs. The popular orchestral or singing pieces seemed to be comparable in length to many of the student films made on campus. The longer classical compositions timed were comparable to the full-length films. Gershwin's composition, *Rhapsody in Blue* has always suggested to me the heartbeat of a great metropolis like New York City. I suggest to the experimenting amateur that he shoot some city scenes to be played with an accompaniment of *Rhapsody in Blue,* either all of it or any part you like. You will discover many things about the relationship between pictures and music of which you have not been previously aware. (See photo 10.)

Even admitting the close relationship between film and music, that does not mean that film is dependent on the older medium. Film is constantly establishing an identity of its own. Several times each year a film comes out in a form that has not been tried before. Examples which come immediately to mind are the films of Andy Warhol, John Cassavetes, Jean-Luc Godard, Alain Resnais.

I have never seen a Warhol film, and the supposed

cinema verité of Cassavetes fails to impress me. But they
have both had the courage to pursue untrodden paths.
The pioneers may not be able to completely succeed in
their explorations, but the ones who follow may well find
some inspiration in the groundwork they have laid.

Films, then, can follow any form the creative artist may
choose. They are entirely flexible. A circus is a form as
is a variety show. Propaganda is a form as is a documentary. When Samuel Goldwyn, a maker of many fine
films, said "If you want to send a message, go to Western
Union," he could not have been more mistaken. Practically every film carries a message. The Russians have long
considered most of our films capitalist propaganda. The
Horatio Alger story form—hard-working boy of humble
origins makes good—is a message film as is the defeat of
the bad guys in almost any Western.

The movement away from the three-act pattern (beginning, middle, and end) is a case of the familiar becoming
lifeless through overuse. A form can become so hackneyed
that as soon as you have viewed the opening scenes you
can predict what will follow. Consequently the film con-
structionist turns to shifting the usual order by using
such techniques as the flashback or a story told in retro-
spect. The recently successful film *Love Story* uses this
technique. We know that the wife has died at the start of
the film even before the two lovers have met.

The conventions of editing techniques have gone
through many changes in the historical development of
motion pictures. When films were new, the shot of an
automobile transporting a leading character through a city
street or a country road was still a novelty. If John decided
that he needed to make a call on Mary, it was thought
necessary to show all the intermediary stages of his getting
there.

A silent picture scenario of this bit of action would have looked something like the following:

[*Interior, John's house—hallway*]: John's butler is helping his master into his overcoat. When he has buttoned it and donned his gloves the butler hands him his hat and opens the door. John exits.

[*Exterior, John's house*]: John comes out. The butler closes the door—John walks toward his car which is standing in the driveway.

[*Closer shot*]: John comes to automobile, opens the door, gets in, turns the ignition key and steps on the starter. The engine starts. John puts the car into gear and roars out the driveway.

[*Street—full shot*]: A milk truck is just passing, the driver has to make a fast swerve to keep from being struck by John's car.

[*Street intersection*]: A pedestrian, most likely with a cane and wearing a silk hat, is crossing the street. As John's high-powered car roars by it splashes mud from a puddle of water onto pedestrian's trousers. He shakes his cane at the retreating automobile.

[*Another intersection*]: John's car swerves as it skids around corner scattering a flock of chickens who retreat in all directions.

[*Mary's house*]: John's car roars up and stops with screeching brakes and a cloud of dust. John jumps out and hurries up walk.

[*Front door*]: John enters, rings doorbell and moves his hands and feet nervously as he waits for someone to answer. After a few moments, door is opened by butler.

[*Entrance hall, Mary's house*]: John is ushered in by butler who takes his hat and gestures for him to enter living
room.

[*Living room*]: John comes in, sits on couch. Butler exits,
John waits impatiently. Soon Mary enters, they embrace, etc., etc.

As time and film rolled by, audiences became progressively convinced that when John visited Mary the means
of transportation was unimportant. Their own imagination could supply the automobile or the magic carpet.
During the next phase of film history, the camera would
show John making an exit from his own home and then
cut to a close-up of his hand ringing Mary's doorbell.

Constant use of this editing convention has eliminated
each intermediate cut until today when John has a desire
to visit Mary we cut from a big close-up of John and his
desire, to John and Mary together without benefit of fade
or dissolve. Most of their clothes will already have been
removed and in something like three feet and fourteen
frames of film they will have landed in bed.

Cutting styles are constantly in a state of flux. I believe
the first time I observed the use of the direct form of cutting was in René Clair's *A Nous la Liberté*. It was a daring innovation which pleased me enormously. I felt that
the movies were coming of age.

One of the questions that arises constantly in editing a
film is when and how to use large close-ups. Big head
close-ups are a most effective accent but I believe that
their effectiveness can be dissipated if their use is over-
done. I remember in my film *Hallelujah*, I tried to stay
away from the use of big heads until we came to a sequence in which their use would be most effective. This
occurred in the scene of religious ecstasy inside the church

when Nina Mae McKinney lured the preacher away from his congregation and into the night woods. The action took place under the observant eyes of members of his family and all the action was enhanced by the use of big head close-ups. Of course, if the director doesn't provide the close-ups in the first place they won't be in the cutting room for the editor to use.

The reverse is also true. A director might shoot close-ups which he hopes will *not* be used unless it is necessary in shortening or eliminating some part of a scene. In times past many producers used to demand that directors cover every part of every scene with individual close-ups. This was requested solely in order to give complete freedom to those editing the film. I was vehemently against the practice as it could double the shooting time of each scene and contribute to the loss of sponteneity in the performances of the actors. I believe that editing should be faced up to beforehand either in the script or on the set. In the case of unforeseen instances where a possible cut would work wonders then the director can get the actors back for a day and shoot only those close-ups that are necessary and will be used. "But the set may be torn down by then," the producer will argue. A background for a big close-up is a very simple thing to arrange and never requires the use of a large set. In confirmation of this, pay a visit to a television studio and see how small a backing is required for most of the scenes they shoot.

The relationship between one scene and another is one of the fundamentals of movie magic. Tempo and rhythm can be created in the cutting room. I used to reject the idea of a movie camera photographing a series of static objects, such as old photographs and statuary, with the hope that movement would be supplied to the finished product on the cutting table, but recently I have revised some of my feeling about this technique. Scenes static in themselves but cut synchronously to a music track take on the rhythm of the music, proving once more that the moving picture camera should never be confined to any restrictive pattern. If a movie camera is utilized for a job for which a still camera at first seemed adequate, but wasn't, all well and good. In this instance, when you put a film strip of a series of inanimate objects into a film editor's hands, consider it one more facet of the medium's flexibility. After all, isn't that what any strip of movie film actually is, namely a series of still photographs? The illusion of movement is injected by the projection machine and the phenomenon of persistence of vision. Why not allow the editor to work with the freedom that derives from the nature of the medium itself?

The film editor doesn't have the same range of freedom in a film shot to a synchronized sound track as he does with one shot M.O.S., (mit-out-sound). The unsynchronized silent film could often completely follow an editor's fancy, but in most instances a dialogue track will govern the film's continuity. If a director's way of shooting is to cover each scene with several angles, the editor's judgment is valuable here. The decision as to which part of which angle to use is of vital importance. Even for those directors who stay with their films through the editing process, an editor with experience and good judgment can make an extremely valuable contribution.

An unfortunate position in which the editor can find himself is after an ideal cutting job has been accomplished: the smoothness of the film's continuity has a tendency to make the editor's work pass by unnoticed. It is like this with many other contributors to a finished film. For instance, consider the work of the set designer and the set dresser. What the audience is supposed to believe is that a given scene is an actual interior with actual furnishings in which the characters in the film play work and live. If the audience is conscious of a splendid set built especially for this particular film, its inherent purpose has failed. It is this way with editing too. One should not be conscious of all the cuts. I often think of this when I drive by an out-door drive-in movie theater and catch a fleeting glimpse of the screen. Because I am not involved in the story or its continuity, I am very much aware of the rapidity of the cuts. In a passing view of the screen that lasts probably less than one minute, I will see six to ten cuts. If I were sitting in what might be properly termed the auto-ence, I would probably be unaware of the rapidity of the cuts.

In my teens when I was studying movies by watching them on the screen, I would sit through a film solely for the purpose of counting the number of cuts. I was amazed at the great number of them. An action comedy could have as many as 150 to 200 in a single 1,000-foot reel. In a drama, there would be fewer but still a surprisingly large number. I would then ask someone, who had gone to see the film for entertainment purposes and not study, how many separate cuts they were aware of in a 1,000-foot reel. They would invariably reply that they noticed about ten or twelve.

Later with the advent of synchronized sound and the wider use of panning and perambulating cameras, scenes became progressively longer. In *The Big Parade,* shot as a silent film and later re-released with a musical and effects sound track, I shot several scenes that ran three and four hundred feet without a cut. This was a considerable innovation at the time (1925) and caused much talk throughout the industry. In one of my sound films, I made a six-hundred-foot dialogue scene but kept it alive with a flowing and changing composition, combining an up and down camera movement (made possible by the use of a small boom) with panning and in and out perambulation.

In sound films, an editor can show his talent in how he handles a large battle or fight scene. In these scenes, many angles and close-ups are shot. These are usually made by a second unit director and crew after the principal director has established the battle or fight choreography utilizing the principal members of the cast. A screenplay might simply indicate "battle scene here" or "fight scene here." The editor has no carefully laid out continuity to follow. He must construct his continuity with only what appears on the screen in the daily rushes aided by references to the detailed notes supplied by the script girl.

I am not saying that the editor cannot be creative in all the other sequences of the film, but there are places that his ingenuity might be limited by the pattern established by the writer of the screenplay and the director. The talented editor often decides whether to use the full shot, the medium shot or the close-up and how long it is best to remain in each of these shots. Through cutting he can be responsible for an unseen rhythm and tempo that can make a film acceptable or not.

When *The Big Parade* (1925) first opened in New York, it was twelve thousand eight hundred feet in length. In the editorial process, we had pared the action to the bone. Each one of the several thousand scenes had been subjected to the closest scrutiny, trimmed to start as late as possible and end the moment the climax was reached while still preserving its full value. Nevertheless, the eight hundred feet seemed to bother the distributing company. They informed us that it made the first show begin too early and the last show too late. They told us that if the New York commuters came out of the theater too late, they missed the train departures and sometimes were forced to spend the night in a hotel in the city. I hated to sacrifice another foot of the film for the sake of eastern commuters, but I began to fear that if I didn't eliminate the eight hundred feet, someone with a less sympathetic pair of scissors might do it for me.

By this time I was directing another film, but I volunteered to take the picture home with me, all thirteen reels of it, and each night after dinner I'd see what kind of loving surgery I could perform. I set up a cutting table in my living room, complete with rewinds and strong frosted back light. It occurred to me after several evenings of getting nowhere that if I could cut three frames from the beginning and end of each scene (six frames at each film splice) the total might add up to eight hundred feet, since there were thousands of splices in the picture. It took several nights and a whole Sunday to do this job. At its completion I still had a hundred sixty-five feet to go. I went back and cut out one frame on each side of each patch and the combined total of the many little pieces of cinema film added up to exactly eight hundred feet. I hadn't cut out one frame over the specified length. Had *The Big Parade* been a sound film, this minute reduction process would have been impossible. Editing would have been constrained by the musical score which could not have withstood the clipping away of a thousand tiny sections. In a much later sound film, a cut of half an hour was ordered by the New York distributors after the film had been in release for a month. I was away from the studio at the time so an editorial supervisor made the eliminations based on possible manipulations in the music tract. Redubbing was out of the question, too many prints had been made and were in the distributing offices. When I saw the film in a regular theater, I felt the film had been seriously damaged in the editing process. I felt that my three years work of writing, producing, directing, and editing the film had been disregarded. I returned to the studio, packed my personal belongings in boxes, walked out, and have never returned.

The editor's craft is a large part of the elusive magic of the medium. Because of this intimate experience with the aesthetic possibilities of the film, conducted within the confines of the medium's practical and technical limitations, the job of film editor becomes one of the most useful stepping stones toward assuming the responsibilities of director. I cannot think of a better one.

The actual architecture of an interior setting or the exact geography of an exterior location does not prevail over the continuity established by the director with the camera or by the editor in the editing room. I recall the time when a prominent director showed me the four-walled set he had built where most of the action would take place for a film he was starting of a famous stage play. As he spoke of his innovation with pride, all I could see was utter confusion if he shot in every direction in the four-walled room. Viewing the film on a screen with its two dimensional character, is not unlike viewing the presentation of a live performance on a theater stage. In both cases the audience is not asked to turn around in their seats in order to see some action against the missing fourth wall which might have been placed in the back of the theater. But because my director friend did use that fourth wall without making any allowance for the nature of his medium, he was unable to preserve the directional force of the original three-walled stage setting, with the result that the completed film was a hodgepodge of confused action.

I have talked about these directional guidelines elsewhere in this book, specifically when I described the staging and shooting of the Battle of Borodino (see Chapter 6). The TV coverage of a football game will serve to illustrate my point. As long as all cameras operate from one side of the stadium, goalpost to goalpost, the objective direction of each team will be preserved. But let one camera move around to the opposite side of the stadium and the established movement of each team will be reversed. If a scene from this one camera is one of action and is intercut with scenes taken from the opposite side of the stadium only confusion can result. Until the advent of color, the direction of movement (left to right or right to left) was the only means of identifying each team. Color has greatly aided in distinguishing each team but the direction of movement should be preserved in its simplest form both in the camera set-ups and in the editing room.

The film maker should be consciously aware of this 180-degree rule throughout the whole field of film action. It is not only beneficial in sports, but in chase sequences, with cowboys, indians and cavalry, animal pursuits, moon landings, dinner-table conversations, and a thousand other movie subjects.

When the moving picture went all out for direct recorded sound in 1928 and 1929, some of the most vociferous objections came from the direction of Russia. Several Russian directors, with Eisenstein as their mentor, had become increasingly aware of the dynamic strength that resulted from juxtaposing images. They thought that the requirements and limitations of an accompanying talk track would stifle and destroy the screen's inherent power. The almost instantaneous replacement of one image with another was central to the expressive potential of the cinema, and had never before been possible with any other medium. And for quite a few years, when film techniques were held dormant by the mechanical limitations of sound recording, their fears were in fact well-grounded.

I would like to quote here some words related to editing as written by the wonderful French master of cinema form, René Clair:

. . . Thus, without consulting one another, the principal masters of the cinema of the time were joining in an opposition that seemed as legitimate to them as it did to me. In their manifesto, the Soviet filmmakers, while approving the use of sound—music and sound effects—declared that "any addition of words to a filmed scene, in the style of the theater, would kill its directorial qualities, because it would clash with the ensemble, which proceeds primarily by juxtaposing separate scenes." Georges Sadoul, in quoting this sentence, correctly adds: "Which was defining editing as the essence of the cinematic art."

Editing is in fact a procedure peculiar to the cinema which has no equivalent in any other medium of expression or art form.

One day I was in a projection room with a five-year-old child who had never seen a film of any kind. On the screen, a lady was singing in a drawing room, and the succession of images was as follows:

Long Shot: The drawing room; the singer is standing near a piano. A greyhound is lying in front of the fireplace.

Close-up: The singer.

Close-up: The dog watching her.

At this last image, the child uttered a cry of surprise: "Oh! Look! The lady has turned into a dog."

Nothing could be more logical and sensible than that exclamation. I would have been quite confused if I had been compelled to reply. Editing is an extraordinary convention to which our eye is so well accustomed that we no longer see what is unusual in it. But for a new eye, one image replacing another in a flash does in fact give the impression of a magical substitution or a lightning-like metamorphosis. [*Cinema Yesterday and Today,* page 146.]

CHAPTER 9

FILM MUSIC

■●

We know that in their day silent films were never shown without an accompaniment of music. Whether the accompanying instrument was an upright piano or a full symphony orchestra, the need was there. Just how much the advent of the sound track did to break up this marriage should be considered here. Films are movement, music is movement; films have rhythm and tempo as does music. Mood is important to the sequences of a film as it is to the sequences of a musical composition. Which is dependent on the other? Which is embellished by the other?

Certainly multitudinous audiences have sat patiently through untold symphony concerts, piano recitals, and jazz groups without feeling the need to watch a film at the same time. In watching silent episodes of a film today how much is the viewer aware of the musical background? Does he feel cheated if the music is not there? Is most of the musical background on television shows and commercials somewhat subliminal like the muzak that goes on endlessly in the corridors and elevators of hotels and office buildings? After a few minutes at each symphony concert I attend, I close my eyes and listen, preferring not to watch the mechanics of the way in which the music is produced. To some, I suppose, the movements and tempo of the conductor, the string, and percussion sections supply a certain visual appeal. But here in the concert hall the music is predominant while in the movie theater it is the other way around. How then may one evaluate the importance of the score of any film regardless of its length or size?

Wonderful names flow into my consciousness: Alfred Newman, Herbert Stoddart, Bronislaw Kaper, Dmitri Tiomkin, Ray Heindorf, Louis Greenburg, Max Steiner, Michel Legrand, Nino Rota, Henry Mancini, Burt Bacharach. These composers and more like them have done their part in adding enjoyment to the great films. How have they approached their jobs?

Unless a producer is trying to develop a hit song in his musical score, the composer rarely joins the picture during the shooting of the film. Generally he must wait until the first rough cut is ready before he can see the film. At this point he sits with the director or the producer in a projection room and the parts of the film that will need musical scoring are discussed and eventually decided upon. This will give the composer an opportunity to work out his themes while the final editing of the film is in progress, approximately one or two months.

At the moment when the final editing is completed a black and white dupe print is struck off from the cutting print. This is given to the composer for his use. From now on his scoring and arranging must be measured in split seconds to conform to actual film time.

He might be ready at this point to play some of his themes for the producer or director for their approval but he will usually add the comment that it will sound quite differently when it is orchestrated.

Here, the composer faces his greatest problem: whether to go all out for the fulfillment of everything he knows about music, making musicianship his goal; or to bow to the dictates of the completed film, which is being interpreted for him by the director. A compromise is not the answer. Instead a harmonious combination of both media must be sought. He must consider that the orchestrator will be thinking in terms of musical sounds and may not be aware of some quiet dialogue that might be made inaudible by a big show of brass. When this occurs the director who will be supervising the final mixing process must suppress the music track in favor of the spoken words. The suppression of the music track in turn causes havoc with orchestral fidelity. Consequently it is best, if possible, not to have the composer present when the final mixing is taking place.

It seems that a sound recording can take only so much instrumentation at one time and still reproduce with clarity and definition. I have long been an advocate of a few instruments at a time on a sound track. This conviction goes back to records and radio broadcasts of Guy Lombardo and his Royal Canadians. I can still hear the vibrato of his clarinet which so effectively identified his music.

One of the best scorings of a film that I remember was done for a Russian picture using only a flute and a bass. It had a quality so articulate that the content of the film has faded from my memory but the music has not. From the viewpoint of the director I wonder whether this is a good achievement or not. It so happens that the composer was Shostakovich. Possibly, it would be difficult to put any music of such excellence in a secondary position to the visual component of a film. Can you recall the impact made by the film *The Third Man* in which most, if not all, of the musical accompaniment was done by a Viennese musician and his zither. Non- movie buffs everywhere were humming the "Third Man Theme" and this original treatment contributed greatly to the success of the film. Then there is the whistling marching song from *The*

Bridge on the River Quai and going farther back, the gossips theme used in Griffith's *Way Down East*.

I myself have on occasion stopped the full orchestra and let a lone harmonica take over. In this way a love theme could be effectively imprinted on the consciousness of an audience. This treatment was used in my film *Ruby Gentry* with the result that the very popular song "Ruby" was recorded by twenty or more best-selling singers or orchestras.

As early as *The Big Parade* (a silent film but with a full orchestra in the pit) I managed to stop the orchestra and let the muffled beat of a single bass drum accent a suspenseful march into no-man's land. Full orchestral scores were composed and sent out with the film. These were written in New York City after the distributing organization had received their first copy of the film. I was unable to get over my idea to the New York group but in Hollywood at Grauman's Egyptian Theater the lone drum beat proved most effective during the long run of the film.

The problem the composer has today is to determine just where music is helpful in complementing the film's content and where it is simply icing on the cake. Too much goo can spoil the cake and it is therefore necessary for the director to go to great lengths to explain his goals and purposes to the composer. If communication is desired by both parties and proceeds unhampered, a wonderful marriage can result. If not, the film can be hurt immeasurably without the film maker realizing it. There is an indelible oneness about music and film of which both the film maker and the composer must be aware. I have proven this natural affinity hundreds of times. It must be observed well and handled carefully. The results can astound one when true integration is achieved.

If the director can film some parts of his picture without the use of constant dialogue he has the option of using a musical or sound effects track, or a combination of both. Sometimes an effects track seems to present the challenge of making a freer use of the imagination than does the usual spoken dialogue track. Voices and scattered lines can be used but they do not have to synchronize with any one actor's lips. Rather they are used to embellish the overall effect of the scene. This treatment works well in combination with musical scoring at points when the unfolding story is not dependent on words. I have used this treatment on several occasions with good results. Two that come to mind are the pursuit in the swamp sequence in *Hallelujah* and the ditchdigging sequence in *Our Daily Bread*. (See photo 19.) In the first instance we were forced into it because there was no portable sound equipment available and in the second I wanted to dispense with sound recording equipment as an economy move during the seven days required to film the episode.

To illustrate my feeling about the importance of musical scoring I budgeted twenty percent of the total cost of the film to the music. The making of the film cost $100,000 and the music $25,000. I don't believe that such a high ratio of music to production cost is prevalent today.

I had first worked with Alfred Newman, the composer of the music and the conductor of the orchestra on *Street Scene*. Because Mr. Newman was regularly employed by the studio and there were no other films in production, he was able to spend much time on the set during the shooting giving us a chance to exchange ideas as the picture went along. The result was his *Street Scene Suite* recorded on discs at the Hollywood Bowl by the Los Angeles Philharmonic Orchestra.

I believe we can say that the composers of music for films today are the Schumanns, the Strausses, the Tchaikovskys, the Dvoraks, of yesterday. As stated before, Shostakovich has written a number of scores for films as has

Leonard Bernstein. I am not saying they are all Beethovens, Brahms and Bachs but who knows what they might achieve were they not so busy earning so much money at their craft.

I first became impressed with the importance of musical accompaniment with the great films of D. W. Griffith. I remember the tender melody from the opera *Mignon* which the orchestra played whenever Lillian Gish was on screen in the Griffith film *Hearts of the World*. More recently I recall the love theme from Zefferrelli's *Romeo and Juliet* and I marvel at the great contribution of the love theme to the success of the film *Love Story*.

When the director Victor Fleming left the incompleted *Wizard of Oz* to direct *Gone With the Wind*, I inherited the job of finishing the picture. At first I was not too happy with the chore as I felt that all the preparatory work done on a film gave the director a chance to establish, by building and rejecting, a solid foundation upon which to operate. Here I was assuming command of an important production on a notice of 24 hours. I admit I was a little apprehensive, that is, until I heard the prerecorded tape of Judy Garland singing "Somewhere Over the Rainbow."

For many reasons which I will not attempt to enumerate here, practically all singing scenes done in major motion pictures are photographed to prerecorded sound tracks. This gives the singer an opportunity to concentrate on voice quality without worrying about facial expression and acting at the same time. It also aids the conductor and the sound technicians to achieve a perfect balance between singer and orchestra. Moreover it gives freedom to the director to have his performers move with an abandon that would otherwise be impossible.

Many of the singing scenes photographed up to that

time had been static and dull. This was my opportunity.
I was able to move Judy around with complete freedom.
And I felt her escape from the boundaries of stationary
singing added to the joyousness of her face and movements as she sang with perfect tonal quality a thrilling
rendition of "Somewhere Over the Rainbow."

I didn't ask for any screen credit on the film for taking
over the last three weeks of production. Victor Fleming
was a good friend of mine and besides I don't believe in
split credits. Much of the important work on a film is
done in the pre-production stage: casting, sets, locations,
script, costumes, characterizations. So much has been
settled beforehand that a second director who comes in
for a few weeks has had much of his work done for him. I
was delighted to be able to make a contribution to this
timeless film.

I can't say that music needs pictures to complete our
understanding and enjoyment of it but I do know that.
cinema embraces all the arts and brings them all to her
ample bosom.

CHAPTER 10

LIGHTING

$\boxed{\bullet}$

During the first years of Hollywood movie making all interior sets were built on open stages. The only source of lighting was natural daylight. A complex of wires overhead were strung taut from a framework of tall poles and timbers placed at both sides of the stage. A series of white and black curtains called diffusers were moved by lines which were controlled from the stage floor. The white material was used to diffuse the sunlight that might find its way into the set, the black cloth was for darkening the set for night scenes. At first no artificial lighting was employed to supplement the daylight. Instead white and silvered reflectors were placed in front of the set in such a position that they caught the sunlight and reflected it into the set from a lateral angle rather than an overhead one. The diffusers were jockeyed about so that the sun struck directly upon the reflectors but not into the set itself. (See photo 14.) Quite often (the wind blows even in California) diffusers would develop holes and tears causing streaks of sunlight to bounce around the walls of an interior setting suggesting the possibility that the elegant living room had no roof over it which was certainly the truth. In these emergencies, stagehands had to climb up the complex rigging to either plug the hole or mend the tear. It helped if a grip had had previous training on a square-rigged sailing ship.

Contrary to the prevailing myth, it occasionally rains in California, too. To meet this unusual situation large tarpaulins were brought out and thrown over all the furnishings in the set. If the walls became water-streaked in the downpour, electric heaters were used to help them dry quickly. Sometimes actors returned from their dressing rooms to perform on water-soaked carpets and sit on soggy, upholstered sofas. If the rain persisted, as it sometimes does, the cast and crew were sent home to await further instructions. I remember one time when it rained for thirty days. Hollywood was at a standstill; actors began to tighten their belts. I seized the opportunity to write a two-reel comedy that could be shot in the rain. I sold it to the old Vitagraph Company for thirty dollars—my first sale of a movie script.

These inconveniences and delays were costly to the producing companies and the practice of building interior sets on open stages was doomed to obsolescence. But the construction of closed stages was not accomplished until waterproof tarps large enough to cover the entire outdoor set were tried. It was then necessary to illuminate these darkened interiors artificially. No specific lamps for motion picture lighting had been developed so it was necessary to import some from the legitimate theater for use in the illegitimate business of movie making. These open arc lamps were called Kleig lights and their glaring white flood of intensive light was only softened by a polluting mist of carbon dust which soon filled the atmosphere of the set.

An actor working all day under Kleig lights would usually suffer the pains of hell in his eyes by nightfall. If his eyes were bathed in soothing cold compresses until midnight the chances were that he would be able to see clearly enough to reach the set by nine the next morning.

Yielding to the inevitable, two types of closed stages

were finally built. Thomas H. Ince in Culver City wanted
to keep out rain and direct sunlight but he was reluctant
to completely relinquish the abundance of natural daylight that Southern California had to offer. He built the
stages of his Triangle Studio (later Samuel Goldwyn Productions, eventually Metro-Goldwyn-Mayer) with glass
sides. When sound came in and stages had to be sound-
proofed against outside interference these glass sided
stages were reconstructed. Both the overhead diffusers and
the glass skylights were hangovers from the early portrait
studios.

The other types of rain- and sun-proof stages that were
built were massive barn-like structures that admitted no
daylight whatsoever. If you entered one of these caverns
when someone had forgotten to leave a light burning, it
would have been worth your life to try to find a light
switch.

The sets constructed on these stages were lighted by
huge banks of Cooper-Hewitt mercury vapor lamps. They
moved across the stage on overhead tracks and were lowered down to the set by steel cables wound on electrically
controlled winches. These banks of purple lights cast a
weird glow over the set until the arcs or incandescent
lamps were turned on. I was making a film written by the
best-selling sex elucidator of her day. Elinor Glyn seemed
to write about sex in terms of time units. Her most popular novel was entitled *Three Weeks,* another *Her Moment,* and the one I was making, *His Hour.* The authoress
was a constant visitor to the set making little innocuous
suggestions concerning insignificant details that would
never have registered in the camera. When the yellow
lights were burning her gums appeared perfectly normal.
Then the arcs would go off and suddenly the gums would
turn a deep purple, almost black. If I were talking with
her, my eyes would suddenly shift to the strange transfor-

mation occurring in her mouth. The contrast was so sudden and startling that it was impossible to avoid the shift of eyes to her mouth, nor the surprised expression on one's face. She couldn't help but notice and her hand would go up to cover her mouth in embarrassment. Apparently the pigment of her artificial dentures had not been pre-tested for naturalness under the unnatural illumination of the Cooper-Hewitts.

After a while the overhead mercury lamps were abandoned and were replaced by glass-diffused arc lamps mounted on mobile pedestals on the stage floor. These were called "broads" and were positioned on either side of the camera and aimed toward the set. With this general fill light taken care of the cinematographer could go to work with spots for molding, for highlighting and for accenting faces and objects in the room. (See photo 16 for indoor lighting rig; photo 12 for outdoor.)

The first consideration in modern motion picture photography is to provide sufficient light on the subject to create a reflected image on the film. This is generally referred to as *fill light*. The ramifications of this basic idea are endless. There is no exact rule for lighting a scene. Again it is a matter of interpretation.

The second principle of lighting is to create the illusion of depth and roundness, to give a three dimensional effect to a two dimensional process. Two dimensional because the ordinary camera has only one eye and shows only height and breadth. But through *cross-* and *back-lighting*, a figure or an object can be made to appear at a distance from its background and this will give the feeling of depth.

For some reason, color photography seems to achieve more of a three dimensional effect than does black and white. It is no doubt because of the color separation and the greater intensity of some colors than others. Therefore, the rounding effect achieved through light placement is not as critical in color photography as in black and white. In the latter the photographer has only the shadings of grays to give a feeling of depth.

The third important principle of good photography is the *key light*. The key light is a basic light. It is generally placed in a raised position on the opposite side of the camera from the fill light. It should accomplish its purpose but generally its effect should not be obvious. It is closely related to the *source light* which is usually set at a brighter intensity than the key light. The light-meter reading is taken from the key light which should be in a 1 : 2 or 1 : 3 ratio with the fill light.

It is possible in some situations to use the source light as a key light. When they are both used on the same scene, the source light will be more apparent than the key light. It was discovered a long while back that it was not necessary to show the source of light when composing the lighting of a scene. If it means something to the scene, then establish it, but if not, don't bother about it. No one watching the film will wonder where any of these first three light sources originated.

I am all for simplicity in lighting or in anything else. I believe that most artists will agree that simplicity is the most difficult thing to achieve. On quite a few films I had these words stenciled on the ladders, grip boxes, and camera platforms used on my set, KEEP IT SIMPLE, as a reminder to the technicians.

In the early days of Technicolor, because of the increased amount of lighting required, the budget and the shooting schedule were increased by twenty-five percent. Then one day I attended a kind of jam session luncheon with a group of film directors in London. One director made the remark that he had discovered that he could shoot faster in color than he had previously been able to in black and white. Surprisingly, others present agreed with him. I decided that it was because color photography is more acceptable under flat lighting conditions.

In one of my films, *H. M. Pulham, Esq.,* made in black and white, I observed that Ray June, the chief photographer, was using thirty-six small spotlights in an attempt to outline every object in the set. It was a simple home library set with only two performers. Later when June did a color TV sequence for me he lit a set of equal detail with a total of five lamps. Time was of the essence but the color scene looked just as good as the black and white.

While the top Hollywood cameramen were painting and molding their scenes with light the top film comedians had a mode of lighting all their own. For fear that some bit of action might get lost in a dim spot on the set, they used a type of flat, straight-on lighting that eliminated all shadows.

One time when I was visiting Charlie Chaplin on his set, he was all ready to shoot when he asked his cameraman if his feet were in the picture. Rollie Totheroh, the cameraman, said that the set-up cut Charlie at the knees. Charlie then told them to move back to include his feet, whereupon all lights and the camera were pulled back a sufficient distance. The change of a complete set-up took not more than three minutes since all the lighting was flat. Had that been a dramatic film, the photographer would not have been ready until an hour later.

On one of my films I had the script girl time how much of each hour I used in directing and how much the photographer used in lighting. The result throughout the film was fifteen minutes for the director and forty-five for the photographer. On many scenes the ratio was ten minutes for directing, fifty minutes for lighting.

I believe that in the lush days of Hollywood, set lighting was too complex and its importance over-emphasized.

Often the number slate was photographed with only half the lights turned on. When I saw this modified lighting behind the number board in the rushes, I would tell the photographer that that was the way I preferred the lighting. But it seemed they were caught up with certain rigid standards of lighting quality and it was difficult for them to break the habit. Gregg Toland did it on *Citizen Kane* and helped make a big name for himself and for Orson Welles.

CHAPTER 11

SPECIAL EFFECTS

■•■

At the Metro-Goldwyn-Mayer Studios, there were two departments that made important contributions to each film. They were not generally publicized because of a studio policy that was against exposing the secrets of trickery in which these two departments were involved.

The first of these contributors to the magic of·film was called the Newcombe Department. This studio was presided over by a sort of genius named Warren Newcombe who had perfected the knack of painting the part of a scene which was directly above the action. His skill lay in matching his painting to the part of the scene where the action took place which was then photographed against a constructed background.

There is another process called a *traveling matte* which permits a substitution of a background *behind* the actors or action but this was not Newcombe's forte. He usually painted the top half of a scene, saving the studio thousands upon thousands of dollars in construction costs. Let us say, for example, that the script called for two mounted riders to cross a drawbridge over a moat and enter the gate of a large castle. The art department needed only to build the drawbridge and the entrance arch as high as the rider's head. Newcombe would supply the castle walls and the castle in his painting, duplicating the direction of light and shadows that were registered on the lower part of the scene.

This is how he operated: for any shot Newcombe would send one of his own cameramen to the set. Newcombe's crew would bring with them a particularly strong platform (or parallel) about six feet in height. The first requirement for any shot of this sort is that the camera must be rock-steady. (Otherwise the combined footage would subsequently show a weaving effect between the two exposures which would destroy the illusion.) As a further precaution guy wires and turnbuckles were fastened from the tripod-head to the top of the parallel to insure the camera's steadiness.

About three or four feet in front of the camera, a clear frame of plate glass was set up. During a rehearsal of the action, the camera operator would mark off lines on the glass just above the highest point in the action. Then he would paint all areas above these lines with a flat, black opaque paint. A dark cloth, or housing, was arranged over the camera and the glass frame to avoid reflections and illumination of the glass. The scene was then photographed in as many takes as the director required.

Before the actual shooting of the scene, the photographer would have ground off 200 feet of test film. This test film would be developed and printed along with the daily rushes. In his studio, Newcombe would put a frame of this film in his camera and project it onto a white cardboard. In this maneuver, he could see exactly what he had to match. When he had finished with his painting, he would use parts of his unexposed test film to verify his own work, and when all was "Go," he would expose the approved action takes.

When I run *The Big Parade* today, I can see bombed upper stories of French farmhouses and the tall height of a cathedral-hospital that I know were not built for the film. This is how I know they are Newcombe shots.

Today with Europe only hours away by jet, and the expansiveness of the large screen, the director would probably insist on going where the action was rather than risk the chance of detection with a Newcombe shot.

With the development of less grainy film and the resultant progress in producing high-grade dupe negatives, Newcombe was able to eliminate the blacked-off glass in front of the camera. The photographer would shoot the scene just as it was, full aperture. The matting process could all be done in Newcombe's small studio.

TRAVELING MATTES

While Newcombe was confined to supplying the part of the set in which the action took place, a man named Williams was developing a process that could supply the scene *behind* the action. Painted matte shots had to be stationary camera scenes, usually long shots. (See photo 28.) The Williams process could combine camera movement in both the foreground and background, thereby joining two separately made pieces of film.

At first a Williams shot required the foreground action to be photographed against a blue backing. A print of extreme contrast was then made from this first negative. In this high-contrast print, the figures of the performers would look very much like moving silhouettes. These black figures in action functioned as traveling mattes: when put through a step printer with the background negative, these black figures prevented a portion of the new or dupe negative from being exposed; this new negative would later be imprinted with the first action negative. Unless Williams put this new negative through the developing process, it would have had to go through the step printer again for a second exposure of the foreground action. If that particular part of the emulsion had not been saved by the blocking process of the traveling matte, the actors would appear as ghosts in the resultant double exposure. But since the traveling silhouettes have masked or matted that part of the emulsion required by the action, the result is two separate, single exposures rather than the transparent effect of a double exposure.

It was the perfection of image registration that permitted the development of the traveling matte. Each studio developed their own process for combining two negatives, either using a version of the Williams' system just described or working out one of their own.

PROCESS BACKGROUNDS

Foreground action photographed in front of a background screen on which a filmed scene is projected has been the most generally used of all process shots. It has been particularly useful for taking scenes in moving automobiles, trains, airplanes, etc., where the problem of crowding in the camera, lights, sound recording equipment, the cameraman, director *and* the actors became an impractical task. But before sound and the subsequent development of synchronous motors, that is the way it was done. (See photo 4.) I remember one scene I made of two people on the back seat of a moving automobile which called for rain outside. After hooking up a generator truck to supply electricity for the lights and camera, we stationed a property man atop the car with a full watering can to supply rain for the rear window.

As late as 1956, during the shooting of *War and Peace* in Italy, the studio was unable to provide background projection for making traveling shots. The reason given was color and large screen VistaVision. We had to mount the rear section of a period coach on a wheeled platform which was also large enough for an eight-hundred-pound Technicolor camera, four stage lamps, sound boom and operator, director, chief photographer, and camera operator together with an electrician or two. It was a real Rube Goldberg contraption. The foul-up occurred when I learned that there were only 40 feet of track available on which to move the oversized perambulator. In a single run of the track, we could cover a mere two lines of dialogue. Then we had to tow the platform back to the starting point, change the camera angle somewhat and make another take of the next two lines.

Through the windows could be seen the residents of Moscow fleeing the city before the arrival of Napoleon. Instead of a projected background scene that could have been taken by a second unit cameraman on a previous day, it was necessary to employ six hundred extras and have them do their stuff over and over because only small areas were visible between the actors and the curtained windows.

One can readily see how much time and money could have been saved by doing this scene on a process stage.

I mentioned that synchronous motors are essential to the back-projection process. When a motion picture camera is photographing a scene projected onto a screen, it is essential that the position of the revolving shutter on the projection machine and the shutter of the camera are in perfect synchronization; otherwise the camera might be exposing its picture at the moment that the picture on the background screen was blacked out.

This process has been used with two or more projectors projecting pictures on multiple screens. For this adaptation, architectural columns, telephone poles, or trees can be arranged on the set to block out the joints between the multiple screens.

There is a company in Hollywood that specializes in renting cut-away bodies of old and new autos and airplanes especially for use in process background shots.

With the present development of lighter and smaller equipment, there seems to be a move away from the process background. I have seen shots made in a moving limousine, the camera hand-held by the photographer on the front seat next to the driver, the sound man lying on the floor in back with his Nagra recorder and a Sun-Gun lamp somehow affixed to the side just behind the driver. Of course the director, with his script girl and assistant, had to ride in another car and must wait until the next day's rushes to see what he had gotten on the film.

This trend reminds me of the old argument between actuality and realism. Actuality doesn't necessarily always look real and trickery doesn't always look phoney. If the audience becomes aware that the process background shot looks artificial, its purpose is lost. When it is done properly, no one is aware of it so these are not the scenes they criticize; they accept them for what they are supposed to be. I think it would be rather difficult to take a close-up of an actor who had never flown a fighter plane in an air battle over Germany in a World War II story using the new realistic technique of avoiding a process background.

The Nagra Company of Switzerland is making a professional tape recorder small enough to fit into an actor's pocket that can synchronize with the camera without connecting wires of any kind. Still, I would hate to hang my cameraman from the wing of a fighter during an air fight but I suppose it's been done, or will be.

A recent development of the process background shot is done with front projection instead of the usual rear projection. It seems strange that a picture could be projected onto a background screen with actors in front of it and yet not have the background projection scene show on the performers' faces or bodies. Interestingly enough the discovery of this possibility grew out of the development of an automobile bumper-sticker and a material that would deflect heat from fire fighters.

The Minnesota Mining and Manufacturing Company (the 3-M people responsible for much sound-recording tape development and a wide variety of cellophane sticker tapes) had developed a material with such a high reflective value that it seemed to increase the intensity of light projected onto it. Hence it was put to use, as an attention getter on the rear bumpers of automobiles. Then Sherman Fairchild, who developed and built the first automatic camera for the United States Signal Corps, became interested in the material. He collaborated with a Hollywood technician named William Hansard, who had been experimenting with the material because of its adaptability for use in background motion picture photography.

In the Fairchild-Hansard technique, the lens of the projection machine is placed as near the lens of the camera as possible. Because of the extremely high reflective quality of the background screen, the intensity of the projection lamp can be very weak, so weak in fact that the projected image is not perceptible on the faces or clothes of the actors. To the eye, the background image seems too faint to photograph and yet when one looks through the camera lens the image appears with startling brilliancy.

The screen material is made up of one million beads to the square inch and is fifteen hundred times more reflective than the actors, or objects in the set which absorb the projected image rather than returning it to be recorded by the camera. This extremely high reflective value of the background screen makes possible a sharp focus and rich color registration on the negative film.

The process was first used in Kubrick's *2001: A Space Odyssey* and Mike Nichols' *Catch 22*.

As in rear projection, the actors must be lighted from the sides or from raised spots that will prevent shadows of the performers from falling on the background screen. This new method seems to eliminate some of the problems of the rear projection system one of which was avoiding the central light source of the projector's beam. Another problem the new system overcomes is the loss of image clarity caused by the projected light having to penetrate a semi-opaque background screen.

MINIATURES AND SPECIAL EFFECTS

Whenever a director is faced with some seemingly insurmountable production problem, he turns to the special effects department to come up with the answers. For example, a full scale reproduction of Captain Bligh's *Bounty* (used in *Mutiny on the Bounty*) sat in a tank of water on one of the stages at M.G.M. One man operating a few levers could make the ship roll to either side or pitch fore and aft with giant waves breaking over the bow and flooding the deck in a foot of water.

Arnold Gillespie was the ingenious head of this department. One of his most impressive feats involved a troublesome scene in my film *Northwest Passage*. Major Rogers (Spencer Tracy) and his group of rangers would come to a dangerously rushing river which they would have to cross without losing any of their men, firearms, ammunition, food, or supplies. In the book and script when they study the possibilities, Tracy suggests forming a human chain by having the first twenty men lock arms. The last man at either end would secure the chain by wrapping his arm around a tree on the bank. In this way, they could protect the whole group who could then walk across (the water up to their armpits), while holding the supplies well above their heads. Had it not been important to me to actually show the principal members of my cast going through this scene, I could have employed a group of expert swimmers to do the stunt. But to take the risk with members of the cast would have been foolhardy. The problem I put to Gillespie was to take the group across a rushing river five feet deep without the risk of accident.

In Idaho on location, I took the lead four or five men into the current as far as they could safely venture. Later, in the studio in Culver City, a large pool was converted into a round tank with an island in the center. Using one half of the tank only, the two banks of the location we had used previously in Idaho were duplicated. The round shape of the tank made it possible to install a series of marine engines and propellers that would drive the water past the cameras at even a greater speed than that of the Idaho river. But what about the danger to the cast? Although they were to work in over five feet of water, if anyone was forced from the chain by the strength of the current he traveled only a short distance, where the depth suddenly slanted up to a shallow two feet. Because of these and other safety precautions, the actors performed their parts without fear. During the many takes, some of those comprising the chain actually did break away but were subject to no more danger than a swimmer being suddenly projected into the shallow end of a swimming pool.

In the M.G.M. film of *The Good Earth*, the script called for shots of swarms of locusts so thick that they blackened the Chinese sky. Gillespie photographed swirling coffee grounds in a water-filled glass jar to achieve the needed effect.

In my film *The Crowd*, I wanted the camera to look at the busy entrance of a high-rise New York office building then tilt upward to reveal its height and at the same time travel up the building to the twenty-first floor. At this point, the camera would select one window and, moving ever-closer to the window, would appear to go through it to an elevated long shot of a large interior of 200 desks. At each desk a clerk would be seated performing the mechanical routine of his job. The camera would continue to move from the long shot, without a cut, down to one man about whom the story was concerned. This shot was planned in 1928 before the days of large camera booms or zoom lenses.

On location in New York, with a hidden camera we photographed the entrance to a large insurance company building at 8:45 in the morning. Hundreds of employees moved through revolving doors on their way to work. I started the camera on its upward tilt to show the stark symmetry of the structure. The trick department constructed a miniature twenty-one-story building about twelve feet high which was laid flat on a stage floor. Over this a camera bridge on wheels was rigged, which permitted the camera to move upwards to the selected floor. Then a windlass arrangement lowered the camera close to the one window behind which was a lighted, still photograph of the 200 desks with the 200 clerks. (See photo 15.) A lap dissolve to the interior long shot made it seem as if the camera had passed through the window.

A large camera boom would have come in handy here but at that time it was only a dream in some ingenious craftsman's mind. Instead, we hung a platform large enough to hold a camera and two cameramen from overhead tracks which were installed to support banks of Cooper-Hewitt lights. At that time these lights were used for black and white photography. An electrically controlled windlass on each corner of the platform would lower the camera while it tracked forward over the sea of desks to the close-up of our one clerk. One can readily see how useful a zoom lens would have been on the exterior shot and a large boom on the interior. I hesitate to suggest a zoom lens for the interior shot for the reason that a zoom shot and a boom shot, though they seem similar, are not the same. A boom shot changes peripheral perspective as it moves forward but a zoom shot does not. The close-up zoom image is still viewed from the perspective of the long shot.

CHAPTER 12

COLOR

⊡

Just as many directors expressed reluctance in accepting the introduction of spoken dialogue, feeling that it was a blow, a retrogressive step in terms of the aesthetics of film making, so it was with the transition from black and white to color. Even today there are those who, with certain subjects, reject the use of color: for example, *The Last Picture Show* which was nominated for eight Academy Awards.

The term black and white is just that—a term, a designation. Non-color film would be more precise: it is a far cry from being merely black and white. The designation was probably true for the earliest films when the blatant contrast in the negatives did not provide for subtle gradations in the prints. In later years, however, Metro-Goldwyn-Mayer held to a practice in their laboratory that made it impossible to achieve any blacks on the screen. They wanted all their films to look soft and sophisticated. They thought the intrusion of any blacks or whites would make the scenes look as if they were shot by a newsreel crew. I remember once when Mervyn Le Roy was so determined to have some London night scenes look really black that he had two cameras on each set-up and had all the film from one of them developed and printed by a laboratory away from the M.G.M. lot.

In modern black and white photography all the colors

are there but expressed in shades of gray. If a painter in oils duplicated every color on his canvas exactly as it existed in the scene before him, he would not be considered a very good painter. Picasso had his blue period. The simplicity of achieving an effect predominantly in shades of one color says something fundamental. A film maker hardly has this choice—unless he works with shades of gray. Several top cinematographers, among them Leon Shamroy and Lee Garmes, have experimented with putting transparencies of one color on each lamp on a set. I know of one instance in a big musical number of an M.G.M. color film where only black and white was used in costumes and decor but it is not usual for a director to be able to control the overall color language of a scene. Antonioni has tried it with some success, as have others, but it is not a generally practiced function of the director.

The word "panchromatic" on black and white film means that the emulsion is color-corrected to be sensitive to all colors. Originally, with less sophisticated film, all reds photographed as black, and blues didn't photograph at all. Actresses making-up with certain shades of red came on the screen with black lips and a black splotch on each cheek. In one of my early short films I used a young Jewish comedian whom I had discovered performing in a second-rate vaudeville theater. He was too young for the part he was assigned to play in the film so he arrived on the set with his face made up with many lines to simulate age lines and whiskers. But he had used a blue pencil to make the transformation. We usually shot the whole film before we were able to see any of it on the screen. The young man of twenty, aging to a grandfather of seventy, came on the screen still a robust twenty—none of the blue lines had registered on the film. Negative emulsion today has been developed until all major colors have their photographic value. Thus in black and white photography, we are seeing color identification whether we are fully conscious of it or not.

In approaching my first film in Technicolor, I soon became aware that the selection and coordination of the color values of the various components of a completed film would have to be determined by an experienced and trained eye. Years of thinking in terms of black and white didn't exactly make me fit for the job. There was no such artist or consultant provided for on the company payroll. The set designer would have his feelings about color; the drapery man his; the costume and wardrobe people theirs; and Mother Nature with her blue skies, green shrubbery, and brown earth colors would blithely dominate the landscape in most scenes. But there would be no specific overall color effect, no control or continuity as a painter would have planned in starting on one of his canvases. I realized that a movie director must now add to his bag of tricks a knowledge of the uses and meaning of color. I resolved to undertake the study of oil painting and I hoped it would not be too late.

From my viewpoint the most productive means of study is by trial and error. Learn from your own mistakes. I was working on the screenplay of *H. M. Pulham, Esq.*, with the book's author, John Marquand, when I was told that my next assignment would be a large color film. Just as in silent picture days we directors thought in terms of pantomime, facial expression and gestures, so in black and white days, except for those paintings we bought for our homes or went to view in art galleries, we didn't do much thinking in terms of color.

I discussed color awareness and appreciation with Marquand who had done some amateur oils on his own. He said as soon as they were dry enough, he put them in a lower bureau drawer and never let anyone see them. I thought that if I could at least learn some of the techniques of painting I would have quite an advantage over Marquand because of my long experience with composition through the finder of a camera.

When the screenplay of *Pulham* was completed John Marquand returned to his New England haunts but not before leaving a field box of paints and brushes on my desk. Inside was a note, my only source of instruction at the time. It read, "Dear King: Don't forget to put in the background first. Good luck. John."

I bought books and learned the names and values of all the colors: Indian red, cadmium yellow, burnt sienna, ultramarine blue, raw umber, raw sienna, etc., and I started to paint. If I encountered an insurmountable problem, I would turn to some more experienced friend, like Joseph Von Sternberg, for help. I had previously bought two oils by Diego Rivera and when he came to my home to see how they were getting along in their new abode I asked him about teachers. "Stay away," he advised, "develop your own style."

I learned about cool colors and hot colors, transparent ones and opaque. I already had a fair sense of perspective but I have never been able to draw. Whenever I wanted to be specific with an art director, an assistant, or the director of a second unit, I wished I had the ability to present my thoughts in a graphic form. However, this inability did not hinder me in my painting. But this book is about movie making not oil painting.

A director must have some familiarity with every art and craft that goes into the making of a film. He must never allow himself to be completely dependent on some other fellow's decision or judgment. There must be, for best results, one conception of the entire film. A basic explanation of many poor films is that the project, though usually started with the best of intentions and integrity, simply gets diluted and polluted along the way.

My first color film was *Northwest Passage* (1940) based
on the book by Kenneth Roberts. Most of the scenes
were about a group of rugged fighting men called Roger's
Rangers. The script called for the soldiers to be dressed
in uniforms of an indeterminate green that would help
conceal the men from their enemies' view as they walked
or crawled through the mottled growth of the forest.
When the production tests were made, I was surprised
to see that what seemed an inoffensive shade to the eye
appeared on the screen as a brilliant Kelly green. I con-
sulted the Technicolor representative, pointing out the
great change that had occurred in the costumes on the
screen. He said that he was aware of it, but that the
Technicolor process was similar to lithography; as for
this particular green, it was one that Mr. Darryl Zanuck
liked and had selected for one of his Twentieth Century-
Fox productions. With some argument and persuasion
we succeeded in getting the Technicolor company to mix
up a new batch of green dye. I realized that the whole dramatic intent of a scene could, through the use of color,
be heightened, diminished, or completely destroyed.

For my second Technicolor film *American Romance*
(1944) I planned an epic story of the European immigrant
in America, his contribution to the great industrial giant
which, at the time of World War II, gave this country
its formidable strength—all the while thinking in color
as well as in pictures and words. For the iron-mining episodes at Mesabi we would confine ourselves to the earth
colors: browns, Indian reds, blacks, heavy grays, and
earthy greens. The light, bright blue of a clear sky would
be avoided at all costs. Blue skies would be used at the
finish of the film in conjunction with the gray-blues of
airplanes and the lemon-yellows and brilliant orange
shades of California which would serve to give an emotional color lift at the end of the picture.

In the first part the metal ore would look like dull

red earth, just as it appears straight from the mine before the heating and refining processes are begun. Then, when we saw the metal again, being rolled from glowing ingots, the flaming reds and red-orange hues would predominate: the birth of iron in the baptism of fire. Bessemer converters would pour out a skyrocket shower of brilliant sparks as the baser substances were consumed and the iron became steel. In Detroit, we would follow the steel as it was transformed into gears, pistons, cams, and crankshafts. Here color would dramatize the cool precision of American craftsmen; the colors could be as articulate as a polished ball bearing.

Then as our American traveled westward to retire in California we would get to know the colors of Rushmore Memorial in South Dakota, the warm adobes of New Mexico, the painted deserts of Arizona, and the concrete masses of Hoover Dam, of orange trees and the dramatic brilliance of the Pacific Ocean. I wanted the film to be a true panorama of America.

San Fernando Valley—a contemporary ranch style home surrounded by orange trees with a background of snow-capped mountains. [*Then World War II and the call for men with production know-how. The first assembly line for turning out big bombers as if they were Fords and Chevies.*] The aluminum wings and fuselages, the wartime workers in blue coveralls, women riveters in white jumpers. The colors ever lighter, cooler, hopeful, until the first complete bombers roll shining out of the factory minute by minute and finally the sky is filled with squadrons of giant planes—glistening aluminum against a bright blue cyclorama.

It was the first film that I know of to tell a color story which paralleled and reinforced the dramatic progression.

It was a big effort but badly sold to the public. It passed with little notice except with the army and navy where it was shown in camps and on battleships and received with enthusiasm. It could have been that we had too many documentary scenes and those who make the big decisions didn't know how to categorize it. But we are speaking of color. I don't remember that my face was red, nor my feelings blue, nor was it a black period in my career so we will move on to other subjects.

III TOWARDS THE NEW CINEMA:

Social and Technological Changes

■

CHAPTER 13

THE WIDE SCREEN AND ITS DEVELOPMENT

●

In 1930 both M.G.M. and Twentieth Century-Fox came out with the idea of wide screen motion pictures. M.G.M.'s process was called Realife Grandeur, Fox's, Magnascope. M.G.M. used a 70mm black and white negative, photographing with a specially built Mitchell camera. In the laboratory the 70mm image was reduced in size so that it would go onto a 35mm positive print. The miracle of this reduction process was that it enabled the 35mm image to be enlarged to a far greater screen size than if it had been originally photographed on the conventional 35mm negative. The objectionable graininess was eliminated by the transformation. Use of 35mm prints in theater projection meant great facility in using standard equipment.

However, certain accessories were necessary to adapt 35mm projectors to the Grandeur format and only theaters with a proscenium large enough to install the large screen were eligible for the change.

The Twentieth Century-Fox system used 70mm in both the negative and print processes, making it necessary to install entirely new 70mm projection equipment for showing these special films.

Because only twelve theaters in the United States were

equipped for projection of M.G.M.'s Grandeur format, the picture I was making was shot with both 70mm and 35mm cameras. It became strikingly evident as soon as we saw the first exterior rushes that wide screen was much superior to 35mm. During the shooting of *Billy the Kid* (1930), my debut on the wide screen, we went on location to the Grand Canyon. In 70mm, the Grand Canyon looked very much as it does when personally viewing it while the 35mm process could not reproduce its magnificent scale in three dimensional values; we were delighted to discover this startling, stereoscopic characteristic of the wide screen format. The reason for the difference was that the wider screen more nearly approximated the scope of vision of the human eye.

Because of the great expense of equipping the theaters with these new projection machines, larger screens and so forth, the exhibitors began to complain that the new technique was economically unfeasible—doubly so because they were still paying for the installation of sound equipment. Sound had been introduced about a year before.

At the time Joseph Schenck was president of Twentieth Century-Fox and his brother Nicholas was the head of M.G.M. These two powerfully positioned brothers apparently got together and decided that the wide screen process should be abandoned in spite of the enthusiasm shown for it by the public. The Mitchell company had by then made many 70mm cameras but they were put in mothballs to await further developments.

Fifteen years later while I was making *Duel in the Sun* (1945) I encountered one of the officials of the Mitchell Camera Company in the studio commissary. He told me how many of these 70mm cameras he had in storage and added that he would like to be able to do something with them. He then proposed that if I could think of some way to utilize them he would give me a large financial interest in our mutual enterprise. The idea occurred to me that there had never been a large screen picture in Technicolor and that the exhibitors who had complained so loud and long in 1930 over the cost of the wide screen, should no doubt have had time in the interim to pay for their sound equipment.

I decided that a western film with many spacious exteriors would put this new medium to the proper use. I started looking for a good story although at the time I was in the midst of doing the rather grandiose *Duel in the Sun*. I felt that I should wait until I finished shooting *Duel* so that I could really concentrate on finding a new script to be shot in wide screen and Technicolor.

Shortly thereafer, the first Cinerama film opened in Hollywood. It was a tremendous success and inaugurated, with its wide screen and peripheral vision, a new era in film production.

As a reaction to the overwhelming success of Cinerama all the studios immediately went to work reviving their old equipment and wide-screen systems. M.G.M. brought out its Grandeur process again and Fox rallied with Cinemascope. The new squeeze process viewed in the theater had a great deal of width but seemed crowded in height. Hollywood pundits dubbed it "the Band-Aid ratio." Paramount also jumped into the act with VistaVision—a process that necessitated new cameras in which the film passed by the lens sideways and horizontally instead of perpendicularly, thereby utilizing twice the standard width.

Then came Todd-AO with which the picture *Oklahoma* was made; then Super-Technicolor which was brought on location in Italy where we were doing the final scenes of *War and Peace* and which we used for several test scenes. The studios were all trying to simulate the wide screen value of Cinerama. Cinerama was photographed on three negatives and then printed on three film strips which were later projected by well separated projection machines running synchronously. The screen image covered 146 degrees (horizontal viewing angle). The dividing line between the three separate pictures was never completely eliminated from the screen, though another company later developed an improved three-camera process which claimed to be able to remove the telltale dividing lines.

Today the wide screen panic of the forties has calmed down to seven variations in addition to Cinerama:

35MM CAMERA

(The Academy aperture ratio is set at 1.33 to 1)

1. (Wide Screen) four perforations; non-squeezed.
2. (Cinemascope and Panavision 35) four perforations; squeezed.
3. (Techniscope) two perforations; non-squeezed for four perforation squeezed release prints.
4. (VistaVision) Horizontal; eight perforations; non-squeezed.
5. (Technirama) Horizontal; eight perforations; squeezed.

65MM CAMERA

6. (Todd-AO and Super Panavision) five perforations; non-squeezed.
7. (Ultra-Panavision 70) five perforations; squeezed.

The following description of Cinerama is quoted from *American Cinematographer Manual,* Second Edition:

Although the triple camera is no longer used, films made in this manner are still shown. The three prints are projected interlocked, from three separate projectors onto a deeply curved screen composed of vertical overlapping strips that recreate a picture of very nearly human vision to viewers seated near the center of the auditorium.

It is now customary to shoot a picture for Cinerama release with a 65mm camera having lenses with a 1.25 squeeze ratio as per Ultra-Panavision on a single piece of 65mm negative. From this, negative prints are made optically on a standard 70mm release print film for single film release with one projector only on the deeply curved Cinerama screen.

As for 16, 8 and super 8mm I have heard of experiments in using an anamorphic lens to squeeze a widescreen picture onto a 16mm frame and then unsqueezing it in projection, but I have never seen it demonstrated. If a 35mm picture is reduced in the laboratory onto a 16mm frame, the film would permit a greatly enlarged picture in contrast to the one photographed with a 16mm camera. This practice is in general use as most of the films distributed by the larger 16mm distributors were originally photographed with a 35, 65, or 70mm camera.

CHAPTER 14

DOCUMENTARY FILMS

Motion pictures fall into two major categories, the so-called entertainment film the structure of which is generally based on some variety of emotional conflict and the documentary film which is primarily informative or educational but which can evoke an emotional reaction and most certainly can be entertaining.

In Robert L. Snyder's book on Pare Lorentz the definition of the documentary film is quoted as given at a meeting in Czechoslovakia in 1948 of the World Union of Documentary:

> . . . all methods of recording on celluloid any aspect of reality interpreted either by factual shooting or by sincere and justifiable reconstruction, so as to appeal either to reason or emotion, for the purpose of stimulating the desire for, and the widening of human knowledge and understanding, and of truthfully posing problems and their solutions in the spheres of economics, culture, and human relations.

Lorentz himself has defined the documentary as "a factual film which is dramatic."

John Grierson, the father of English documentary films, refers to them as "The creative treatment of actuality." I can think of no better analysis of documentary film making than that given by G. Roy Levin in his introduction to his book *Documentary Explorations:*

Grierson . . . felt that documentaries should be used for purposes of propaganda. Paul Rotha, a very respected documentary film-maker himself and the author of the standard text on the subject, feels that documentary films should have an ameliorative social purpose and that they should be produced by groups rather than by individuals with egocentered sensibilities. Many of the French see little difference between documentary and fiction; rather, they see each as a personal, artistic expression. Some Americans tend to see it as an impersonal and objective gathering of data. Many would see social purpose as a necessary ingredient.

At best, a definition of documentary is like any definition of an ongoing form of art: useful in indicating its concerns and raising provocative questions, but limiting and therefore falsifying. If one wishes to discuss the subject, the point is not to tie it up with string and lock it up in a box, but to be stimulated and perhaps to learn something. Suffice it here to say that the main attributes of documentary as generally understood are: it treats reality, past or present (or future), either by direct recording or by some indirect means as compilation or reconstruction; very often it is concerned with social problems, which means, almost by definition, such subjects as the poor and the alienated. . . .

It is impossible to build a fence around documentary films: subjectively they embrace every activity. Because of their scope, and often their spontaneity, they are most often photographed with a hand-held camera. The lighting can be haphazard, realistic, natural, or non-existent; the print can be grainy, overexposed or underexposed. Any of these characteristics might suggest the old-fashioned newsreel, an example of the early, classic documentary.

I started my movie career as a newsreel cameraman. I got my first assignment to cover the largest movement of troops in American history even before I had had access to a movie camera. But under pressure I found one, and the film I shot became part of a newsreel called *The Mutual*

Weekly that was distributed throughout the world. In Texas, my home state, I made short films for the sugar industry and a Title Guarantee company. Later I shot travel footage for the Ford Motor Company which produced a newsreel that was distributed free to the theaters.

When I arrived in Hollywood I became conditioned to the fiction film, or should I say entertainment film? For a long period of time I thought only in terms of drama or comedy. Lengths varied, but not the general approach we used along the way.

Then one day Robert Flaherty's *Nanook of the North* (1922) burst upon the Hollywood scene with its real people building real ice igloos in real, frigid, northern Alaska. The film was showing in regular theaters and people were standing in line to see it. I am not a film historian so I don't know what else was going on in the world in the field of documentaries at that time. However, I can report on its effect upon Hollywood. We realized that it was possible to make a film without the complexity of a studio, without constructing a long list of sets and furnishing them, and that it was not necessary to depend on New York- or Hollywood-trained actors to play the parts. Several large studios tried to latch onto Mr. Flaherty and put him under their control, but this didn't work out too well. Bob Flaherty was a snow goose who found it impossible to soar high with his wings clipped.

I cannot point directly at whatever proliferation resulted from Mr. Flaherty's first films, but his influence was certainly felt. We started sprinkling our fancies with actualities. Soon the pasty white make-up on actor's faces (which often looked like hideous masks when the actor was too busy or too lazy to include his neck) was replaced by faces that required no make-up at all.

Stars who had built profitable careers out of atrocious performances began to slip into oblivion when their

phoney theatrics were compared to the talents of those re-
cruited for the films made by the neo-realists in postwar
Italy. Even decades before, with F. W. Murnau's *Tabu*
(1913) and Cooper and Schoedsack's *Grass* (1925) we were
beginning to discover that facts could be more dramatic
than fiction. The label "legitimate theater" began to make
way for the legitimate appearance of the new films. This
maturing process continued, eventually flourishing under
the creative experiments of the *nouvelle vague* and later
the *cinema verité* directors in the 1950s and '60s.

Quickly I think of Flaherty's *Moana of the South Seas*
(1926), Van Dyke's *Trader Horn* (1931), Bennett and Mar-
ton's *King Solomon's Mines* (1950) and my own film, *The
Crowd* (1928). In this film all scenes laid in New York
City were shot on the actual locations there. Many times
I have heard it referred to as a semi-documentary. The fellow who played the leading role in my film was not an
established actor at all, but a young guy who had been
living the kind of life in New York City called for in the
screenplay.

I began to feel I was developing a style that could in-
tegrate the seemingly disparate styles I had worked with
before: the dramatic, entertaining story line with the realism and credibility of a Flaherty-type documentary. I had
either consciously or unconsciously been moving in this
direction from the start.

Today, when I run my film *Our Daily Bread* (1934) for
new audiences I am always asked if the performers were
real down-and-out people, or if they were cast through an
actor's agency in Hollywood.

On this point I believe that most everyone watching a
film wants to believe that what they are seeing is really
happening, or at least, a close approximation. It is only
when some action or situation is injected that is so grossly
false that, try as they may, they cannot accept it. When-

ever I have seen a film in which I became so engrossed that I forgot all about lights, cameras, microphones, and director, I have reacted with delight and enthusiasm. I remember when I first saw David Lean's *Brief Encounter* (1945). I came out of the theater and on the sidewalk I turned to my friends and exclaimed, "It is hard to believe that there was a photographic and sound crew present at those intimate scenes in the railroad station." Many times since I have used this rule when trying to evaluate a director's work. David Lean reached this height again in *The Bridge on the River Kwai* (1957). To me this kind of anonymity represents the ultimate in dramatic direction and performance; it shows no strong dividing line between the fiction film and the documentary.

I had the privilege of working with my good friend, Pare Lorentz, on *The Plow That Broke the Plains* (1936), *The River* (1937) and *Fight for Life* (1940) in an advisory capacity. What can I say about him to explain or examine his motivations that resulted in these powerful documentaries? I do know that he felt deeply about the need to show interested people what their government must do, and he had the audacity to convince the same government that they should foot the bill for their own enlightenment. Whenever he was stymied in this determination he jumped over officialdom and went right to the top: Franklin Delano Roosevelt. Lorentz used a movie camera as a poet uses his pen. His films had the same ambience about them.

In documentary film production I believe the number one advantage is that the sky is the limit. Correction, the universe is the limit: we have already seen a moon documentary and will soon see one from Mars. I believe that is the way one should approach a documentary. The word is misleading. It comes from *document,* which has a rather dull connotation.

In this country we are deprived of seeing the documen-

tary films made by the United States Information Agency
because of some antiquated agreement made between the
government and the commercial producers and distributors. Here is a fertile field for the discovery and development of capable and talented documentarians. I deplore
the fact that their films are made for showing in foreign
countries only. I believe the people whose taxes pay for
them should have the privilege of seeing them but perhaps
my reasoning is too simple to be taken seriously by the
decision-makers.

There is no such thing as a standard documentary. Each
one is a creation in itself. There is no standardized length,
no camera or lighting restrictions whatever, and the
documentary maker is not burdened by any traditions
from the theater (e.g., the old first, second, and third act
structure); nor is there any pressure to conform to anything previously done in literature.

It is an art purely inherent to the cinema. It is nurtured
and flourishes from within. It has more opportunity to
give originality full sway than any full-length feature film.
A low close shot of a tractor will look vastly different than
a high long shot of the same tractor, so wherein lies the
meaning document?

The American Heritage Dictionary defines "Documentary" as: "1. Consisting of, concerning, or based on docu-
ments. 2. Presenting facts objectively without editorializ-
ing or inserting fictional matter, as in a book, newspaper
account or film. Plural, Documentaries: A television or
motion picture presentation of factual, political, social,
or historical events or circumstances, often consisting of
actual news films accompanied by narration."

Here we go again: *defining* generally turns out to be
confining. Perhaps we should free documentary films with
a new name such as M.O.A., that is, mit-out-actors, para-
phrasing that most descriptive label for a scene shot silent
—M.O.S.

(Let me digress for a moment to explain the seemingly improbable origins of M.O.S. I have seen this symbol used all over America and Europe including Spain and Yugoslavia, and I wouldn't be surprised to see it written on the slates of Japan. When sound came to Hollywood in 1929 the executives at M.G.M. thought they would have to shoot their films in each language of the country in which it would be distributed. Dubbing was a word not yet brought into studio parlance. Consequently, French and German directors were imported along with actors from these countries. When the American director had gotten his OK take of a scene, the foreign director would move in with his cast. One German director with a voice that could carry for a city block occasionally called out, "Dis one mit out sound." One day the slate boy in a facetious mood wrote in chalk on the slate the words, "Mit out sound" and soon these evolved into the abbreviation M.O.S)

You have the camera. Take it and run with it. Hold the camera upside down if you want to, run the film backwards if you feel like it, shoot in color or black and white, or mix the two together if this says something for you. Underexpose or overexpose or throw the lens out of focus. Run at any speed the camera will accommodate and light the scenes with candles and don't pay any attention to what I have to say or anyone else. You are the first person who has ever done what you are doing. No one has ever done it before. You are photographing ideas and feelings, not words.

CHAPTER 15

SIXTEEN MILLIMETER FILM MAKING

|●|

In the early years of film making, there were only 35mm film and cameras with which to experiment and learn. There were several makes of 100-foot capacity wooden-box, hand-cranked cameras available to the amateur and I suppose the cost of buying the negative and sending it to a laboratory for developing and printing was less than a 100-foot roll of 16mm would be today. Thirty-five-mm black and white negative was $3\frac{1}{2}$ cents a foot when I began shooting newsreel shots with my little 100-foot Erneman camera. The cost of developing the negative and printing on positive stock added another $6\frac{1}{2}$ cents per foot so that we could figure on 10 cents a foot for the negative and one print.

Without a synchronous sound track and color to worry about, getting a film from camera to screen was quite simple. When I started making one-reel films in Texas, my partner and I set up our own laboratory for developing and printing in a one-room office. We ran into some difficulty when my partner wound the negative film on the developing rack wrong-side-out so that the emulsion stuck to the frame, thereby removing two frames of picture every three feet. We showed the picture locally and, I suppose, the bright flashes in the theater every few seconds made it easier for late customers to find their seats in the dark.

But we were becoming accustomed to surmounting embarrassing "boos." I remember the time I wanted to increase the speed of the hero's car in an auto-racing film. The car we used could only go sixty miles an hour. I wanted it to look as if it were traveling twice as fast, so I told the camera operator to turn the crank at half speed. He thought I didn't know what I was talking about so instead of cranking at half speed he doubled the speed. This made the lead car seem to travel at thirty miles an hour, instead of one hundred twenty, but it won anyway. You might say the race was rigged.

The race was shot on a beach along the Gulf of Mexico. On the question of setting the lens at the proper exposure for defining the separation of sand, sea and sky, the cameraman also got his signals mixed. Instead of stopping the diaphram down to the smallest opening ($f/22$), he reversed himself and opened the lens. I suppose he was confused by the higher numbers signifying smaller openings and the lower numbers, larger openings. The scene was so over-exposed that there was no separation between beach, water and sky, no emulsion left on the film, with the result that in the theater it looked as if a cockroach (our hero's winning car) progressed slowly across a blank but brilliant projection screen.

Or the time I wanted the heroine cheering for her boyfriend to appear as if she were seated in the midst of a tightly-packed group in a crowded grandstand. We had about fifteen or twenty volunteer extras at our disposal so I told them to sit closely against one another in spite of the fact that on the mornings when we were shooting, they were surrounded by acres of empty seats. To complete the illusion, I told the same cameraman to frame the shot so as to cut every person on the outer edge in half. I wish I had captured on film the disdainful look he gave me as he returned his attention to the camera.

So he allowed a good safe space of three feet of empty

grandstand around the sardine-packed group. I didn't kill him when I saw the scene on the screen. I couldn't, he owned the camera, which was the only one available in the whole state of Texas.

In those early days, we never made night scenes at night with artificial lights; we made them in daylight, then tinted the positive print a deep blue signifying moonlight. Fire scenes were dyed red and sunset scenes were tinted pink and sometimes amber. After I moved to Hollywood in the early twenties, I still went into the laboratory and dipped the racks of film myself. If I succeeded in achieving the exact shade I wanted, this one print would be used as a pattern for all successive prints.

The first hand-held 35mm camera that came to my attention was the Bell and Howell 100-foot capacity Eyemo. The Bell and Howell 400-foot capacity tripod-supported camera was generally used in Hollywood. It had been preceded by the Pathe, which was cranked from behind and was adorned by two black 400-foot wooden magazines perched on top of the box that contained the mechanism; and the Dubrie, an ingenious, beautifully constructed French camera whose two magazines sat side by side inside the rear of the camera. This meant that the film had to go forward out of one magazine and after passing through the aperture perform an about-face and return back to the take-up magazine. The more or less standard Mitchell succeeded in pushing the Bell and Howell out of top popularity.

I believe it was either Bell and Howell or Eastman that came out with the first 16mm camera around 1923. Like the 35mm Eyemo, the power-supply of Bell and Howell's 16mm Filmo was a hand-wound spring that had a capacity of about twenty-two feet on one winding. Eastman's 16mm hand-held was also spring wound as was the DeVry and the Majestic.

The introduction of 16mm had the effect of freeing the

activity of film making and putting the camera and equipment into the hands of eager amateurs who had never considered the possibility before. Colleges began organiz-
ing cinema departments and supplying them with cameras,
projection machines and editing equipment. With the development of synchronized sound, the classes prolifer-
ated as did the number of universities that considered
cinema an important and necessary part of their curricu-
lum. One basis for this growth is the portability of 16mm
equipment versus the weight and cumbersomeness of the
earlier 35mm. For instance, a very good 16mm projector
equipped for sound reproduction can be carried with one
hand and transported in the trunk of the average automobile. Only recently has Japan produced a 35mm projector that is portable, in six cases, that just might fit into
an American car.

With the less expensive 16mm film and equipment the
number of persons who could find the finances to make a
film multiplied by the ten of thousands. By a film, I mean
any kind of a film and any length. Photographic enthu-
siasts made filmed records of their travels abroad and
showed them in their own living rooms. Some were good
enough to show at club meetings and to take on lecture
tours and some were sold for exhibition on television. The
individual had discovered this newest and freest of all
mediums of expression. He found that it was limited only
by the boundaries of his own imagination.

Every subject imaginable has come under the camera's
perceptive eye. Cinema students at the University of
Southern California alone turn out an average of 560 films
a year and the number is increasing rapidly. A program of
the better ones draws audiences that fill a large auditorium for a week. A selected program from this school
and from the University of California at Los Angeles plays

a yearly circuit of colleges in Europe and America. The length of each subject runs from three to twenty minutes with an average of around ten minutes.

There is a *Guide to College Film Courses* published by the American Library Association in Chicago for The American Film Institute. In it are listed colleges where film studies are taught. At the top of the list is U.S.C. with eighty-two different subjects related to cinema. Second on the list is U.C.L.A. offering seventy-five courses. Four hundred twenty-seven colleges in the United States offer one or more courses in film production, film appreciation, film criticism, film history, or closely allied subjects.

The results of the survey taken by The American Film Institute during the 1971–72 academic year show that a total of 2,392 film courses are being offered—1,372 are open to undergraduates, 341 to graduates, 477 on both levels. (The precise data was not supplied for the remaining 202 courses.) In addition, one hundred four schools have film study courses for teachers.

Fifty-seven colleges give Bachelor of Arts degrees in film; 18, Bachelor of Fine Arts; 14, Bachelor of Science; 32, Master of Arts; 19, Master of Fine Arts; 6, Master of Science; 11, Doctor of Philosophy and 3 give an Associated Arts degree.

Among the 82 classes scheduled at the University of Southern California are:

Introduction to Film	Film Directing
Fundamentals of Film	Motion Pic Prod Techniques
Visual Communication	
History of the Amer. Film	Documentary Film
Language of Film	Filmic Expression
Filmwriting	Makeup for Motion Pictures
Photographic Communication	
	Adv. Camera & Lighting

Motion Picture Camera	Photography in Scientific
Motion Picture Editing	Research
Animation	Motion Picture Processing
Art Direction	Basic Screen Writing
Directing of Informational	Photojournalism
Mot. Pic.	Special Effects in Cinema
History of Motion Pictures	Seminar in Mot. Pic. Busi-
Motion Picture Sound Re-	ness
cording	

Besides the universities surveyed above, there are a great number of junior colleges and high schools teaching cinema.

A few advanced students in cinema move on to the American Film Institute Center for Advanced Film Studies which occupies the large castle-like ex-home of a prominent oil-rich family at 501 Doheny Road in Beverly Hills, California. The grounds surrounding the building are opulent which makes for convenience in shooting a variety of exterior locations. The bedrooms have been transformed into cutting rooms and the larger rooms into offices, conference and seminar rooms. Students are divided into two categories, Fellows and Interns.

As quoted in the center's Film Courses Guide:

The Center is at the heart of AFI's effort to build an American tutorial tradition in film. The two year program is individually designed to meet the particular needs and capabilities of each of the forty Fellows who may elect to study writing, directing, cinematography, or theory and historical research. The Center's program is open to talented men and women who are filmmakers and scholars in the early stages of their careers. No academic degree is required. However candidates must demonstrate in their application a basic level of technical proficiency and experience in one/or more areas of filmmaking or film research.

A limited number of Auditors to the Center Program are accepted each year for 3 month periods. Auditors participate in the regular weekly program and participate in Fellows' production projects.

A short while ago, I ran my film *Our Daily Bread* for cinema students at the University of St. Thomas in Houston, Texas. These students were working entirely in 8mm and super 8mm film and equipment. There were several shelves of film classics in 8mm prints available to them. A lightweight 8mm projector could be borrowed and taken home overnight along with one of the available classics. The student operating the projector could stop the film whenever he felt like it, study the composition or lighting of a single frame, back up and re-run any scene he wanted to study carefully or run the whole film as many times as he liked. Think of the advantages these students enjoy over the pioneers of film making. Hardly anything the early innovators did had ever been done before. However, there is another side to this agrument: Knowing that there is no precedent, no established method, an artist may be more uninhibited in his work, freer to follow the dictates of his inspiration. I recently received a letter from a student fan asking me to name someone who had had the greatest influence on my work. For an opener, I wrote "David Wark Griffith" but then I realized that Griffith would have to take second place. The person who influenced my work more than anyone else was King Vidor.

I am convinced that the great surge made by the French New Wave group and the reason it persists is the availability of a full range of worthwhile films, shown daily at the Cinemathèque Français in Paris for a modest fee. This is not to take anything away from the penetrating explorations and originality of the New Wave directors but one can see continual evidence of influence by the great films of the past in their work. And why not? If something is good it is generally always good and the same goes for bad. Someone once said that the aging of an inferior wine doesn't make it into a superior wine. The same is true of films.

Merritt College in Oakland, California, has a film making program for handicapped youngsters. Here is a quote from a letter I received from the director of the program, Don De Nevi:

> I have enclosed a copy of a new Cinematography program I am developing for my Junior College: A program to re-cruit and train hard-core ghetto youth in film making. My thrust will be directed toward all youth of poverty who have never held a camera before and simply make film-makers out of them. Perhaps a new brand of urban directors could be fostered whose sense of social urgency would be like yours. In any case, it's the first kind of such a program in the Junior Colleges of America and I aim for nothing less than channeling that raw, often primitive and certainly innocent way of seeing (among poor black, brown, red, yellow, and white youths) into films of teaching—teaching about man, his hopes, his visions, and goodness. In other words, the creation of films similar in spirit to *Our Daily Bread* for the 70s and 80s.

Millions know of fades and dissolves, of long, medium and close shots, of A.S.A. ratings, of booms and dollies, of baby spots and barn doors, where only a handful did before. Credit most of it to the revolution and evolution of 16mm. What better way can a man find out about himself: He searches out a subject, he photographs it, and then sits back and calmly evaluates what he has done. There will always be many surprises in store for him. A friend of mine, a prominent psychoanalyst, used to visit me on the set from time to time. Often he commented how much my work resembled his. I was never quite sure of the similarity until later I heard interviewers say that there were certain distinguishable threads which ran through all of my films. One evening in Aspen, Colorado, I saw two films that I had made ten years apart. I saw definite character changes in myself in that ten year spread but above all, looking back over fifteen years at both films, I was able to trace a psychological continuity of which I had hardly been aware before.

Sixteen millimeter film makers began to attach cameras to trees where they took close scenes of the intimate home-life of birds; they put them into snake pits and explored the sex life of insects through microscopic lenses. Naturalists and forests rangers in isolated outposts became film makers. The world and everything in it became their studio. Then one day, the 16mm camera went beyond the earth with our space explorations, and then onto the moon.

In 1964, I bought a 16mm Beaulieu camera in Paris. As an exciting supplement, I equipped it with two zoom lens, a 17 to 85mm Berthiot, and a 12 to 120mm Angeneux.

I had never worked with a zoom lens and I wanted to feel out its possibilities. At first, I shot scenes around Paris and in every one I utilized the zoom action of the lens. Of course, I overdid it, but I wanted to become accustomed to the effect.

When I returned to California I thought, "Here I have a camera and enough money to buy all the color film I need and pay laboratory costs. What will I shoot? I don't have to sell anyone the idea in order to get finances and I don't even have to consider the mass audience appeal. I can write the script myself, operate the camera, and speak the narration."

Equaling my interest in cinema has been a lifetime interest in Metaphysics. One evening, I started by putting a yellow tablet before me and sharpening some pencils. Two hours later, I had written an eight page narration for a short film (25 minutes) to be called *Truth and Illusion: An Introduction to Metaphysics.*

From a graphic or pictorial point of view, many of the lines of the narration were abstract. Here was a new challenge in film making and a most interesting one. What do you photograph to illustrate a line of narration that reads:

The primary meaning of metaphysics is derived from the discussions by Aristotle which deal with the nature of being, with cause or genesis, and with the existence of God.

Because of the experimental nature of this film I had determined to avoid animation and specially constructed shots. Every subject had to be available to the amateur film maker without excessive cost. Participating actors, where necessary, would have to be friends, or those volunteering for the fun of it. Take a line like,

Nature gets credit which should in truth be reserved to ourselves, the rose for its scent, the nightingale for its song, the sun for its radiance. The poets are entirely mistaken; they should address their lyrics to themselves and should turn them into odes of self-congratulation, on the excellency of the human mind.

There were obvious subjects for photographing nature—a rose, nightingale, the sun, a poet's hand writing with quill pen—and maybe I could think up some abstract way to visualize the human mind.

Permeating my thoughts each day throughout all other activities was the challenge to translate specific philosophical ideas into images. Often the solution would come after a kind of distillation process in which a series of a dozen indeterminate images came to mind and were rejected. As a result of these mental gymnastics, a line of discovery began developing in my thoughts. For years directors and producers had become offended whenever a writer wrote a sentence in a script describing a character's thoughts instead of his actions. Many times, I have heard a producer take a writer to task by demanding of him something like "Tell me, how on earth can you photograph 'long sought opportunity for retribution?' You can't photograph thought." In the task I had given myself, I could take no refuge in this supposed limitation.

For some years, cinema had been coming into its own as the freest of all means of expression. Must we continue to live under the old restraint that ideas cannot be photographed, only action? What sort of all-encompassing art medium would that undertaking require? Why must philosophical ideas continue to be confined to the written and the spoken word? What might Plato or Aristotle have done with a 16mm Bolex?

Perhaps illustrating a spoken narration is not the whole answer. Perhaps philosophical content has permeated more full-length films than we realize. The answer lies in refining the idea and expanding our awareness. As some show-business sage said about movies way back in the early years of this century when movies were still in their swaddling clothes, "The possibilities are enormous!"

I put the challenge up to you, you 16mm film makers. Give yourself the most difficult assignment you can think of. Dream the impossible dream. You will learn more about what a camera can and cannot do than by any other method, and you will learn more about yourself than you thought possible.

An interesting example of developing a camera eye happened while shooting the film, *Truth and Illusion*. I wanted a picture of a swirling galaxy to illustrate one of the lines in the script. Had I been working in a studio or had I a sizable budget for the film, I would have simply gotten in touch with the Special Effects department or the Animation department and put the problem up to them. But I was determined to do my part in setting a course for any amateur.

I had in my bathroom a full-size, open-face tape recorder using seven-inch reels. I used it to listen to French instruction tapes while dressing. One morning as a ray of sun slanted in through a window, it struck the two slowly revolving reels of the recorder and reflected a pattern on the bathroom wall that revealed the moving galaxy for which I was searching. To replace the wall covering of the room, I scotch-taped a sheet of plain blue cardboard to the wall, moved my camera in and waited until eight o'clock the following morning.

I was amazed at the many examples of light phenomena that I began to see everywhere. On window shades, on tree leaves, on the surface of pools of water, even swimming pools. All reflective surfaces are constantly creating moving patterns when you look for them.

The film, when finished, was eight hundred and seventy-eight feet and ran twenty-four and one-half minutes. As originally intended, I have only shown it to groups with which I am acquainted. It has been requested by about a dozen universities, among them Stanford University, Massachusetts Institute of Technology and California Institute of Technology. I showed the film and gave a talk at Cal Tech where all the studies have heretofore been in the so-called "hard sciences." The new class which saw the film was called, "Aesthetics of Cinema and Music and Beyond," certainly no designation for a group which was not ready to understand the film. The discussion following the showing was lively and provocative and served once more to convince me of the close liaison between aesthetics, metaphysics, ontology, and cinema—and I am not going to be one to exclude the "hard sciences." In fact, I am not going to exclude anything.

As of today I have had no offers for general distribution to the public. There is bound to be a vast difference between the interest of the audience en masse and the specialized one. However, at times I have believed that if an artist speaks with clarity and sincerity, being primarily honest with himself, it is possible to interest everyone. After all, we are all of the same life and mind.

Throughout my career I was always taking exception with those who said such and such an idea would be over the public's head. This seems to me an attitude of gross arrogance. The difficulty probably stems from the fact that the idea is over the film maker's head or the one who wants to block its inclusion in a film.

Lillian Gish, a long time friend, after viewing my short film insisted that it should be released to the general public. This is still an open question with me. Probably the larger the audience, the lower the norm. That is why the small theater chains serve such a useful purpose. I can't believe that Ingmar Bergman, when planning one of his films, is thinking of filling a huge auditorium of three to five thousand seats.

Sixteen millimeter films can be made with a thousand goals in mind. To mention a few: teaching, travel, tourism, industrial research, selling, experimental, television, learning by doing, scientific, medical, educational, entertainment, technical explanation, agricultural studies, wildlife, political propaganda, space exploration, oil exploration, geographical studies, geological, surgery, and sports.

For more detailed technical information on 16mm film making I suggest turning to several excellent books on the subject. *Guide to Filmmaking* by Edward Pincus is published in paperback at $1.50 and gives information on

8mm vs. 16mm film, cameras, lenses, raw stock, filters, sound recording and editing. As I have said in some other context, technicalities, while tremendously important, are by no means the whole picture. We want to find the whole film maker here, why settle for less?

The following anecdote is revealing in terms of my own development over the years and the awareness I have gained about the untapped potential of cinema as an art form.

At one time during the era of silent films Sergei Eisenstein, the renowned Russian director, arrived in Los Angeles. For the sake of simplicity I am tempted to say Hollywood instead of Los Angeles, for Hollywood, although it is a geographical locality, is also a word for a large community of people engaged in various capacities but all in the same field and with overlapping interests. Soon after I had met Eisenstein he asked me if I would like to see his latest film, *The Old and the New,* a copy of which he had brought with him. At the time I had a projection booth in my home equipped with two projection machines for running silent films. Eisenstein said that if I didn't have a regular operator to handle the projectors, his cameraman, who was in his party, would be happy to offer his services. That evening he and his group of three associates came to dinner at my home.

Afterwards we ran his new film. At the beginning of reel three, as I remember, (all reels were in approximately 1,000-foot lengths at that time and all professional films in 35mm) Eisenstein jumped up and started waving his arms in front of the projected light beam calling, *"Nyet— Nyet!"* loudly enough to be heard by the cameraman-projectionist enclosed in the fireproof booth. After a few moments the picture rolled to a stop and the cinematographer came out of the booth. Then an argument in Russian ensued which was translated for us as it went along. Eisenstein was insisting that his friend had put on reel number four instead of reel three. The cinematographer was just as insistent that it was reel three he was running and not reel four as Eisenstein contended.

After a flow of Russian expletives, which most of us didn't understand, Eisenstein stood his ground and demanded that his cinematographer take out the reel and put the next reel on instead. The cinematographer, realizing defeat, did as he was told. The picture proceeded towards its conclusion as the great Eisenstein remained quietly in his seat.

I have no explanation whatever for this incident. If the film itself was a film with a chronological story line instead of a succession of meaningful images, it is most unlikely that the confusion could have occurred. From the viewpoint of progressive storytelling, with which I was imbued at the time, I couldn't tell the difference between reel three and reel four (nor perhaps between reel five and six had I been asked to decide on the proper sequence). It was just that kind of film. I would certainly like to see it again today from the perspective of all that I have experienced and learned in the interim.

CHAPTER 16

FILM FESTIVALS

●

Many people have asked me what goes on at a film festival and why. Basically a festival is organized to provide an audience for film makers whose aesthetic goals venture beyond box-office and financial considerations. Hollywood is oriented to the next film, the next job, buying or selling a story or screenplay, staying on a studio payroll as long as possible, financing a film production or putting a package together. However, the Cannes Festival (France) is considered very much of a market place inasmuch as there is an international audience partially made up of film buyers who are there to discover an interesting film to be distributed in their home country. At other festivals the acceptance of a film for showing in competition or any other purpose means that the film will be given a certificate of entry and the right of distribution in the country in which the festival is held. So film festivals do not totally accent film aesthetics. They do have their commercial side as well.

I have attended quite a number of film festivals, principally in European countries. On some occasions I have served on the jury that is responsible for awarding the prizes at the close of the festival.

1956 *Cannes Festival (France)*
      Invited Guest

1962   *Berlin Festival (Germany)*
       President of the Jury

1963   *Locarno Festival (Switzerland)*
       Invited Guest—Retrospective showing of my films.

1963   *Aspen Conference (Colorado)*
       Invited Participant—Two of my films shown.

1964   *Edinburg Festival (Scotland)*
       Delegate of U.S. State Department
       (Received Golden Thistle Award)

1965   *San Francisco Festival (California)*
       Invited Guest—One day devoted to different direc-
       tors, films shown.

1969   *Moscow Festival (U.S.S.R.)*
       U.S. Member of International Jury

1970   *Venice Festival (Italy)*
       Invited Guest

1970   *Sorrento Festival (Italy)*
       President of Italian–United States confrontation.
       Retrospective showing of my films.

1971   *San Sebastian Festival (Spain)*
       President of the Jury—Retrospective showing of
       my films.

Besides the opportunity of seeing films from all the countries of the world when I have served as a jury member, the thorough analysis and discussion of the merits or demerits of each film shown have given me insight about the thinking of each member of the jury. In nearly every case their principles of judgment have transcended both personal and national bias. Usually the decision is unanimous which points to the fact that political or geographical considerations don't actually exist. Purely artistic, philosophical or technical achievements dominate the discussions and guide the jurors in their selections. I have seen a film with strong box-office potential suddenly drop from consideration when a juror pointed out that it contained a number of insincere scenes, obviously inserted for their effect but which destroyed the unity and integrity of the film.

At the first meeting of the jury, the director of the festival usually gives a brief talk about the guidelines we should follow. These stress that the films are to be judged solely on their artistic merits. The jury is told that there are no political issues to be considered and favoritism to any country must not be thought of.

At the Berlin Festival in 1962, I was elected President of the Jury by the other jury members. The most difficult job of the jury is to see all the films accepted by the festival committee. It means seeing three and on some days four films. All must be either in the language of the country in which the festival is held or have superimposed subtitles in that language. This means that if a Japanese film is entered in the Berlin Festival the dialogue sound track will be in Japanese and the superimposed titles a translation into German. Imagine the plight of an American juryman who can understand neither of these languages, and yet has to give an honest and perceptive appraisal of the film. A translator, understanding both German and the language of each jury member, is supplied, but seldom is she fluent enough in her second language to keep pace with the film's dialogue, nor articulate enough to be well understood by the jury member.

The various films from all countries—countries as diverse as Mongolia, Taiwan, Pakistan, Nigeria—come at the jury so rapidly that you have to keep a detailed record of what you have seen. Otherwise, after two or three days, the whole spectrum would become a photographic jumble, laced with polyphonic dialogues. Twenty-three films later, you must be able to deliberate on the individual merits of each film in a sincere and impartial manner.

At the Berlin Festival, of which I was the President, and in that capacity repeatedly echoed the democratic instructions of the festival director, I was surprised at a small incident which occurred at the final event in which a German senator gave out the prizes the jury had awarded. As I left the stage and walked up the aisle to return to my seat, I felt a hand firmly clutching at my elbow. I turned slightly and saw that my walk was being slowed down by the government minister under whose department the festival was held.

"Why didn't you give an award to France?" he said crossly in my ear, "Didn't you know de Gaulle is coming to Berlin tomorrow!"

In Moscow, where I was not the president but the sole voting member representing the U.S., the same impressive instructions about artistic integrity were given on the day before the film showings began. I went back to the table of the American contingent at the hotel, and in rebuttal of someone who had cynically remarked that the voting was already in the bag, detailed the sincere and impartial instructions we had received. I recited how we had been told that political or ideological boundaries must not enter into our decision-making. Our instructions had come from the jury chairman who was a Russian film director. I felt I almost convinced the American group, one of whom was there representing the United States Information Agency.

During the course of the festival, it is customary for the jury to hold an interim meeting every three or four days in an attempt to eliminate some of the films judged unworthy of consideration. This is done in an effort to make the choice of the winning films and performances less complicated, less ponderous. At these interim meetings, it appeared that the East German entry had failed to impress the jury members; the majority wanted to remove it from contention. However, an argument put forth by the East German member of the jury was so vociferous the film was kept on the list for later consideration.

The final jury meeting was called at ten in the morning following the last showing of films the evening before. All films in competition had been shown in the Palace of Congresses inside the Kremlin walls. Three times daily the jury of sixteen members, each representing a different country, had assembled in a conference room on an upper floor of the huge auditorium building. The theater itself seated 6,000 persons. The Russian public was welcome to come to all showings for a modest fee.

The day of these final deliberations was the morning following the first successful landing on the moon. At breakfast, the waiters and waitresses who served the American table had assembled in a small group to drink a toast to the three brave Americans. All of us at the table seemed only able to respond with tears of gratitude. They were clearly visible on everyone's cheek. As I drove from the hotel across to the Kremlin, my driver turned back and saluted with the only American word he had ever learned. It was "Armstrong."

When I arrived at the jury room, the members were all seated around a television set. We watched a replay of the landing and Armstrong's brief walk. Then a toast was offered saluting the historic event and the courageous Americans. I replied on behalf of my countrymen: "I accept your congratulations, not solely on behalf of my fellow Americans but on behalf of all mankind." It was not until a week later when I read a copy of an American news magazine that I learned that I had spoken substantially the same words as Armstrong.

The moon landing accomplished, we gathered around the long table to start our final deliberations.

The prizes: three gold medal awards, three silver

medals, awards for best actor and actress, and several special awards.

Early voting showed one of the Russian films in the gold medal category but the second Russian film, a black and white entry, ran just short of garnering enough votes to move it into the silver award possibility. In short order, this unacceptable situation was changed by moving one of the gold medal recipients into a special award category, thereby leaving an opening in the top three. This was adroitly filled by moving one of the films in the second place group up into the first group thereby leaving an opening for the black and white Russian film to move a step upward into the silver award group.

But what about the East German entry? A vote was taken —three votes for, thirteen against. This precipitated a forceful oration from the Russian jury chairman. The substance of his speech was that political propaganda could be classified as art just as much as any other subject matter. I had first met this able film maker in California quite a few years before. On a previous trip to Moscow, I had dined at his home and grown to appreciate his friendliness. Here he was pounding the table and using a voice much louder than necessary to the representatives of the sixteen countries around the table.

To me there was only one explanation. During the late night or early morning, while Armstrong and his comrades were negotiating the moon landing, my friend had received a telephone call from someone up the ladder in the festival or cultural hierarchy that must have gone something like this: "The East German film must receive an award."

As far as the chairman was concerned, that settled it. Another vote was taken. This time, it was ten against, six for. His vociferous speech had won three more votes.

He must have been put on the spot. I knew by the films

he made that his heart wasn't in what he was proposing.

It was settled very simply and irrefutably when the jury reconvened after the lunch break; the chairman announced that it had been decided to give the East German film a special award.

I do not consider the foregoing incident typical of most festivals. I doubt if it is even typical of the every-other-year Moscow festival. Moscow alternates with a festival held in Karlovy Vary, Czechoslovakia.

However, I find myself having a hard time overlooking another unethical procedure of which the Russians are guilty. The theme of the festival on which I served on the jury was: For Humanism in Cinema Art, for Peace and Friendship Among Nations.

And yet, on the last night in a documentary film made by North Vietnam a U.S. plane was shown that was shot down by Viet Cong antiaircraft. The shot brought forth big applause from the audience. During these last night showings, another documentary made in Bulgaria was filled with anti-American speeches and sentiment. I don't object to the making of these films but to their being shown in a festival that emphasizes peace and friendship.

As a result of this breach of good faith, compounded with several others that had previously occurred, the U.S. Department of State refused to sanction official participation in the 1971 festival. However, this official rejection did not deter a group of about twenty American film makers from entering some of their films and participating in the festival. Cinema yes, politics no.

In September each year, the Department of Culture and Tourism of the Italian government stages what they refer to as a confrontation. Each year a different country participates and only films made in the one participating country are shown. No jury or voting is needed as it is simply a confrontation between Italian film makers, journalists, government officials, and film buffs with the film making representatives of the participating country.

As in all affairs of this kind, only films which have not been shown in the host country can be entered.

For quite some time, I have been aware that one of the principal sources of subject matter for the screen has been found in the errors and abuses of American life. When expanded to larger-than-life size by a film production, these can be given an importance they hardly deserve. When viewing one of these films in our own land, we Americans seem to rationalize them by attributing them to some small backward community or some historical period from which we have long since evolved. We are inclined to say, "Oh that is about some small backward community in Mississippi where nothing similar has happened in the last twenty years." But this mood of rationalization is not prevalent when one sits with a European audience. Often I have felt like rising up at the finish of one of these films and addressing the audience somewhat in this manner, "The film you have just seen is not typical of life in the U.S. as it is today. If you want to see how things are in America, you will have to make a journey there and see for yourself and not form an opinion from many of our films."

In the next chapter, I will argue against censorship with regard to the use of sex and violence in contemporary films. The apparent contradiction between my thoughts and feelings when participating in a film festival and about film making in general, deserves some explanation. I am well aware that times are changing, that the accepted values of the past—both moral and aesthetic—are in the process of evolution, and I am firmly opposed to any sort of external limitation on a director's choice of subject matter. This is my point of view as a film maker and an artist. However, in the present context, as a juror representing the United States, my role is quite different: it has a *political* dimension. In this situation I feel justified in advocating that a certain amount of control and restraint be used in choosing the U.S. entries.

Imagine my surprise when in the theater of the Royal Palace in Naples on the final evening of the Italian-American 1970 confrontation, Frank Shakespeare, chief of the USIA walked on stage. The following paragraph approximates the substance of his speech.

On the last day of the Sorrento confrontation, the committee supplies a ship that transports all participants of the festival, their families and baggage, to Naples where they are put up at the best hotel as guests of the Italian government. Closing ceremonies are supposed to be held in the beautiful San Carlos Opera House adjoining the palace, but during the 1970 affair President Nixon had decided to pay a visit to the U.S. 6th fleet stationed principally in the Bay of Naples. In a protest move, the Neopolitan Communists had decided to occupy the San Carlos so the closing ceremonies had to be moved into the palace.

Tora, Tora, Tora, the film chosen to be shown at this event, could not be shown advantageously in the smaller palace theater so the evening was confined to passing out honors and speeches, most surprising of which was Mr. Shakespeare's. I voiced my opinion earlier about the freedom to ignore technical exactness in film making but somehow when we spend billions buying questionable friendship abroad the situation of deliberately going about creating a bad image of one's own country is a point that should be seriously evaluated. How can we object to what Moscow does to the U.S. at her festivals when we ourselves are guilty of greater offenses?

At a recent festival in San Sebastian, Spain, I criticized a film because it lacked sufficient movement. Other mem-

bers of the jury pointed out that I had not understood the
dialogue sufficiently—it was in French—to realize that
this was the exact technique such a screenplay demanded.
Each one of them, a director from the Argentine, a film
writer from Czechoslovakia, an actress from Spain, a producer from Paris, a cinema school instructor from Italy
and a director from England explained points that because
of language difficulties I had failed to comprehend during the projection of the film in the theater. The strict
philosophical mood demanded a restraint in action.

It was then that I realized I must build no barriers
around this freest of all artistic mediums. I changed my
vote. Two months later, I saw the film dubbed into English and I realized how right my fellow jurors had been.
My criticism was evidently a hang-over from my silent picture days when pantomime and movement were essential
elements of film, when a film with too many subtitles was
just not good film making.

CHAPTER 17

SEX AND VIOLENCE

Since 1952 when the United States Supreme Court ruled that freedom of the press and the other communications media included freedom of the screen, the entire complexion of film making as related to sex and violence has undergone a startling transformation. This development started long before the abolition of censorship: we could make a long list of silent films that exploited both sex and violence, but the scenes were filmed less openly (and perhaps more provocatively) than they are today.

I am repeatedly asked about the use of violence, sex, and nudity in today's films. The issue hinges upon whether the audience creates the demand or the film makers. It is difficult for me to believe that money-hungry producers would continue to exploit sex and violence if audience dollars did not make it well worth their while. Then too, the immense demands of television, the great number of movies being produced throughout the world, devour ordinary story material at an astounding rate. A young director on his first or second film might do everything in his power to include more shocking scenes than ever before. In this way, if in no other, he can call attention to himself as a more daring film maker than his competitors.

Whenever anyone singles me out to complain about some strongly sex-oriented film I usually reply, "Who twisted your arm to make you see it?" I explain that there are many ways to find out about a film before going to the theater. And the truth is that these people know what the film is about, but afterwards try to rationalize their voyeurism by finding a scapegoat to ease their own conditioned consciences.

Not too long ago it was supposed to be a highly provocative gesture for a woman to lift her skirt and expose her ankle. As for revealing her calf, this shocking exhibitionism was reserved for circus performers and prostitutes. In those days, violence, in the form of war, could only be perpetrated with impunity by an act of Congress; and murder, as capital punishment, by the decision of a judge and jury.

Today's new freedom is a sign of the times, an indication of an era of debunking that has been brought to a head by the obvious phoniness of the Vietnam War. It stands to reason that we cannot expose the hypocrisies of this war without becoming aware of innumerable other hypocrisies we have blithely accepted over the years. After all, nudity and sex have been part of life since the dawn of time. As for violence, observe the dignity and honors showered on the war-makers of the past.

I am delighted that films can be made today that more accurately depict what actually takes place in life, the bad along with the good. Fairy tales are not for me. The truth may be a bitter pill; we will squirm and quake and kick when it is suddenly thrust upon us. But only through finding out about reality can we hope to begin to solve the many problems that beset us. The film medium can help us in this task. It is already beginning to peel off the layers of self-delusion which have so effectively insulated us from life.

IV FILM AND REALITY
■•

CHAPTER 18

THE MOTION PICTURE AND ITS RELATION TO LIFE

In the films I have made I tried always to establish communication with life. At the same time I have avoided attempts by others to tell me when a scene was technically correct or not. Technicalities be damned! Film is an art form and must not be inhibited by anyone else's interpretation of how you might behave or how an event happened. There is no correct interpretation of a historical happening. If there were it might not be useful under the circumstances. Everyone has his own point of view. There are as many truths as there are faces.

When I was making *The Big Parade* I wanted a group of soldiers to pass the camera in a double-file column. The two technical assistants I had on the set were seasoned officers who had seen service at the front in World War I. They objected to my column of two's; apparently the formation had never been used throughout the Eastern Front. I knew in spite of their long service they could not have covered the entire area of American participation. This particular formation served my purpose: I went ahead as I had planned. Later, while running almost a hundred reels taken by the U.S. Signal Corps at the front, I saw thousands of feet marching in a double column. I arranged for a showing of these films and asked my two experts to watch it.

In making *The Citadel* in England, the producer supplied me with a young doctor who was to act as my technical assistant as far as English medical practice was
concerned. The English are mired in technical correctness.
When I would have Robert Donat, who was playing the
lead character, examine a patient, the expert would be
at my elbow with technical criticism: "His fingernails
should have been examined, and his back listened to with
a stethoscope."

And I, desperately: "But you don't understand, this is
not an actual medical examination but a simulated one.
I don't want the audience to get up and leave the theater
while a lengthy diagnosis is taking place."

In another scene Donat was supposed to revive a newborn baby who had stopped breathing by alternately
dousing it with very cold water and then hot water. We
didn't want to take a chance with a live infant. The
trouble with live infants is specifically that they *are* alive:
they move. Therefore, I asked for a safe rubber child. I
told our prop man to get the right dimensions from our
medical expert. When we were all ready to shoot the scene
and the rubber infant was brought forth it looked like
anything but a newborn babe. The doctor swore he had
gotten his measurements from the best medical authority.
It was too late to put off shooting the scene until a new
baby was made. We had to photograph the scene without
showing the baby. Maybe it was better that way.

One of my favorite sequences of all time is the ditchdigging sequence in *Our Daily Bread*. Although this
sequence has been thrilling audiences since 1934, if I
had based it on the advice of a professional ditchdigger,
its impact would be as dull as its name suggests. Its basis
is music. There is nothing factual about it besides the
fact that the men use picks and shovels. They move many

times faster than men would if they were actually digging a ditch to contain the stream of water shown in the film. But it is the crescendo of rhythm and music carrying the viewer along with it that invariably brings forth applause at its conclusion. (See photo 19.)

I wouldn't even approach a documentary film on a factual basis. Facts need to be interpreted. This is where the individual comes into the picture.

Acting is not factual, but life interpreted. I remember some scenes in a film by Robert Flaherty, one of the most respected documentary makers of all times. The film was laid in the swamp and bayou country of southern Louisiana. Flaherty probably thought it would give a feeling of reality if he used local people in the scenes. The result was that the natives didn't appear to be real people at all. They looked instead just like terrible actors, which they were.

The final scene in *War and Peace* (between Audrey Hepburn and Henry Fonda) presented a problem in writing and direction. It is difficult to summarize all that has been said throughout a film of this scope. When I outlined to Henry Fonda the three endings we were considering, in an effort to get a reaction from him that would help in my decision, he didn't like any of them.

I told him these three endings were more or less the way the scene must go.

"I want to tell you," Fonda said, "that I can be a real son-of-a-bitch if you make me do a scene I am not in accord with."

"That's your choice, Hank," I answered. "We are simply trying to end the picture with the best possible scene we can devise. That's our goal. If you, for some reason, don't want to go along with that objective—well I'm sorry."

I forgot to mention that one of the endings had in it a small dog. Fonda said he would absolutely refuse to

play the final scene in competition with a small dog.
(Reminds me of the time Clark Gable refused to kiss a
girl who was not beautiful on the ground that it would
spoil his screen image.)

Di Laurentiis, the producer, a writer, and I worked out
a satisfactory last scene, which contained some of Tolstoy's philosophy, and a small dog, in spite of Mr.
Fonda's threat that he could himself become the son of a
small dog.

The interior of the burned-out Moscow home of the
Rostov family: Natasha and Pierre walk through the ruins
trying to express a note of hope in spite of all the tragedy
that they have experienced. I hoped to appease Mr. Fonda
somewhat by letting the small dog tag along quite unnoticed by either of them. But I was determined he would
speak Tolstoy's words.

In the middle of take one, the recording engineer stops
the take. He comes to me with the information that he
has not understood one word Fonda has spoken. I call to
Fonda (it is a long shot) and ask if he will please speak louder
so his words can be recorded understandably.

Fonda then makes a speech in a perfectly loud and clear
voice to all those assembled on the large stage. It goes
something like this:

"I want you to know that I have made my career on
the basis of realism. I have repeatedly refused to play parts
that were unreal and I have refused to speak lines that
didn't have a ring of truth about them. And I will not
do so now."

The first word I could think to answer was "Balls!" but
I kept it to myself. I picked up the public address microphone hanging on my chair:

"Okay—we'll shoot the scene again the same way, except
this time Mr. Fonda will speak his lines in Russian. We

want to be realistic, don't we? Why are we having Russian people living in Moscow carrying on conversations in
English? Mr. Fonda, play the scene in Russian."

Ready. Lights. Places please. Camera. Action.

Hank must have suddenly realized how ridiculous his
speech had been. He spoke his English lines loud and clear
and the sound man reported that he heard every word.

A film should have an integrity of its own. If it is
adapted from a stage play or a novel, the film maker has
a right to change whatever part he thinks can be improved
in film form over the original. There is, of course, his
allegiance to those who liked the work in its original
form, but on the other hand, if he feels he can make an
improvement, he must consider what percentage of the
average audience has read the book or even heard of it.

In an audience of 1,000 persons, I doubt if over twenty
people have read *War and Peace* or known it well. In
discussions with Americans, before I left and after I
returned, most said that they had not read beyond the
first one or two hundred pages. In Italy, the percentage of
readers was much higher. When I was interviewing
an Italian (or for that matter any other European), I had
only to mention characters' names. They would know immediately who I was talking about. An art director, whom
we later employed, said he had found a copy in a cave where
he was hiding out from the occupying Germans. He said
he had read it through six successive times. The two-volume
edition that I used in planning the film measured 1,665
pages and was well illustrated, a fact I found useful in making the film.

I am a slow reader and I am unable to read any work
of fiction which has a potential for a film without going
through a process of visualization as I go along. I tackled
War and Peace at the rate of fifty pages a day, making

copious notes and underlining useful speeches as I went
along. I traveled to Italy by boat and planned to complete
my preparation the day before arrival. I knew that once
I set foot in Rome, the demands on my time and the
thousands of questions that would have to be answered
would prevent quiet contemplation about which parts
of the book to include in the screenplay.

R. C. Sheriff, the English playwright, was supposed to
be meeting me in Rome with an outline of how he
thought *War and Peace* should be adapted to the screen.
Upon arrival, I learned that Sheriff had refused to leave
the quiet atmosphere of his farm in Cornwall in favor
of a hectic job under Italian supervision in Rome. After
several unsatisfactory replacements I had the good fortune
to enlist the services of Mario Soldati who worked in
close collaboration with me in writing the screenplay.

In making a film of the story of *Billy the Kid*, we had
available old photographs of William Bonney (Billy) and
his friend Pat Garrett, the sheriff, who eventually killed
him. In making a decision on the casting of these two
characters, I was aware that not one person in ten thousand
would be familiar with what either of them looked like.
As far as the role of Billy the Kid was concerned, the
studio had signed a rather colorful football player named
Johnny Mack Brown, and had ideas of making him into
a western star. I had been trying to get a go-ahead on the
project from the studio for three years. When the head of
production said the project would be approved if I would
use Johnny Mack Brown in the leading role, I didn't give
much consideration as to whether he looked like the original Billy or not.

As for the part of Pat Garrett, they wanted me to
bolster the name value of the cast by using Wallace Beery.
Beery seemed nothing like Garrett, but I was thinking

only of the image I had formed while working on the screenplay. How many people living today know what the Lincoln County sheriff was actually like? I hoped Beery's screen image would interest a great many filmgoers, and that its strength would wipe out any script reference to the actual Garrett. It was a gamble, yes, but it proved to be worthwhile.

When a film maker runs one of his films years after it was made, he is able to view the picture as a disinvolved spectator. He can enjoy it, or not, as he will, unencumbered by petty remembrances. *Billy the Kid*, I decided, was a fine motion picture.

CHAPTER 19

WHAT IS A FILM?

▣

Shakespeare said, "The play is the thing." Obviously he didn't know about movies. Today one might say, "The movie is the thing." Whichever of the crafts may scream the loudest that their contribution is the indispensable one, the effect is only a voice in the wind. The big paradox is that film embraces all the arts yet is none of them. The movie is the thing.

I remember an old comedy routine where one comedian went through the first two acts of a musical play asking, "Why is the fourth of July?" Throughout the play his fellow comedian kept replying "I don't know. Why is the fourth of July?" In the last act the first comedian explained his question thusly: "J is the first, U is the second, L is the third and Y is the fourth of July."

It is like that with film. The story is the first—or is it; the director is second—perhaps; the screenplay is third—maybe; the actors are fourth—forgive me; and so on and on until one day it is released and shown in a theater, or in a basement, or on an airplane or in many instances not at all. Something mystical has happened between points one and four or even *before* point one was conceived. From then on everyone keeps guessing: "Why is a film, or why is it the way it is?"

Editing is magic, lenses are magic, locations are magic, actors are magical, lighting is magic and the maestro who blends them all together is the sorcerer. There is no beginning and no end. So what can we say about film making? Everything.

I have seen wonderful films hurt by the photography, by the acting, by the editing. I have seen several of my best films fail at the box-office and yet I know they *were* among my best. They have lived the longest. The box-office means little in the long run. Once when the head of a large studio was talking to me about coming to work for him, he named several of my films which he said would be the kind of films he hoped I would make if an association was consummated. He did not name any of my biggest box-office successes. He named the films in which I had most successfully expressed myself. They were *not* my biggest hits.

Film is life. We can learn about film from many angles. But anything with a touch of the infinite is impossible to circumscribe. Film, like life, can move in new directions without warning; we must be flexible, prepared at any moment for any eventuality. My growing awareness in recent years that God lives within each of us has come to determine the entire future of my professional and spiritual life. Life is like Everest. It is there, waiting to be conquered.

In recent years whenever I have been on my way to some university to give a talk in conjunction with the showing of one of my films I have often wondered why I am not speaking to the philosophy department rather than the cinema department. All my life I have been interested in the science of being: ontology. And this fascination has kept pace with my professional dedication: film making.

En route to participate in a program celebrating the fiftieth anniversary of a community church, I thought over this dichotomy which exists within me. The basis of my philosophy is a belief in Oneness: Unity. I was to dine with ministers and students of theology and yet I would be there to talk of, and answer questions concerned with, the movies.

Why would a church group primarily concerned with theology bring in someone to talk about movies? Perhaps films can help us learn about life and living. Does the chance to watch shadows of ourselves in the speaking dark of a movie house explain cinema's great attraction—an attraction that has survived even the onslaught of television?

Must I, as a director, continue to see films and life as an antinomy? Why must I painfully shuttle back and forth between the real and the unreal? Life is one. I must try to meld the science of being and the aesthetics of cinema. Only by doing this can I hope to evolve a comprehensive and viable philosophy of film making.

In previous chapters I have often spoken about the mark of the individual on the integrity of the film he makes. Is this individual integrity the answer to the integrity of liv ing? How else are we to express our humanness? How else are we to express God?

Ayn Rand wrote a book which she called *The Fountainhead.* The theme was the infinite integrity of the individual artist. I made the film. In it Gary Cooper played an architect. He had designed a building for a housing project and while he was absent on a vacation cruise someone took it upon himself to change the facade of the buildings. Upon his return he tried in every way to restore the construction to his original idea but was unsuccessful. It was then that he decided to dynamite the face of each building.

To me this seemed a preposterous and impractical solution. I went to Jack Warner, the head of the studio, with the argument that if, when the picture was completed, anyone changed or edited some part of the film and I retaliated by destroying that part of the film, would he forgive my rash action. He replied that he would not but that a court judge might. This was the case in *The Fountainhead* book and screenplay.

I lost my argument but it was a victory for the artistic integrity of Roarke, the character Cooper was playing. I don't believe I am ready to advocate destruction as a means of achieving artistic integrity; but it does make a point. It has been said that destruction is sometimes just a name for construction—two sides of the same coin.

I remember the opening shot in a documentary film about the Tokyo Olympics. A large office building disintegrated to make way for a superhighway which would lead to the new stadium. Destruction gives way to construction. A matter of viewpoint and judgment.

What has all this to do with film making? Everything. It is your world. You do not *see* it through the lens of a camera, you *make* it with the lens of a camera. You don't see *with* the eye but *through* the eye. This is why today's cinema is a great and articulate medium of expression. For years it was only considered a form of entertainment. Its recognition as a powerful art form came slowly. The struggle is still going on. It will be won, if only because the cinema is the only complete art form. The more complete, the more expressive the medium. As Marshall Mc-Luhan put it: "the medium is the message."

Not all media can support the impact of individual reality. The definition of the word solipsism is the theory that nothing in the universe exists outside of one's own consciousness of it. The film maker's decision is comprised of what goes out through the lens, as much if not more than what comes back through it. As Dr. John Dorsey of Wayne State University defines it; "Only in my conscious subjectivity can I recognize, realize, and exercise the truth of the inviolability of the wholeness of my life. . . . To attain this desirable emotional development I must cultivate my feeling of being a whole, unified individual so that it can become my ruling passion."

This discovery of cinema as medium for expression is the reason for its rapid proliferation in schools and universities. It can free the individual spirit like nothing else. This growing awareness of subjective reality partly accounts for the revolution of thinking among young people today. They have discovered the reality, and the divinity of the subjective approach. No amount of pressure from outside authority can invalidate their findings.

Why has cinematography contributed so greatly to this growing awareness? Because it achieves a protean, plastic simulation of life through controlled illusion. This ability to imitate all aspects of human living tends to expose the deception, the sham, the hypocrisy of *non-cinema* everyday living. Through its ability to enlarge and amplify and focus and select, the cinema holds life still for a painful examination. Insincere love scenes and sentimentality in some old films are the first to crumble under the critical gaze of today's young audience.

Cinema has evolved a new world. Materially it is a world of illusion. Spiritually it is a world of reality. We have analyzed the mechanics of cinema to find that it is no more than a series of still photographs that are projected with a rapidity that gives the illusion of movement. This is exactly what occurs when we observe any movement with our living eye. So, even from a mechanical basis the illusion of movement may be no more illusory than life itself. From a philosophical viewpoint, good cinema presents a mirror to life. Our lives, passions, fears, hates, and prejudices are all reflected in glorious technicolor on the silvered screeen in triple-giant size. Our weaknesses are revealed, our violence exposed.

All the world is a stage. It takes cinema to make you aware of it. In so doing, the cinema can help free man's soul and expand his consciousness.

People are weary of being *told,* they want to *see.* Attempts to limit the language of cinema have never worked. Those who try will be destroyed by its power. I am not speaking of a future revolution. The revolution is here.

INDEX

235